Ounces of Philosophy in a World of Ads

Gilles Vervisch

Ounces of Philosophy in a World of Ads

Collection Essais-Documents, Paris, 2023
www.maxmilo.com
ISBN : 978-2-315-01262-6

For Louise

"Outside, even through the pane of the closed window, the world seemed cold.
In the street, small gusts of wind spiraled dust and torn paper. Although the sun was shining and the sky was a hard blue, everything seemed faded, except for the posters stuck everywhere. From every major crossroads, the face with the black moustache stared back at you. There was one on the opposite wall. BIG BROTHER LOOKS AT YOU," repeated the caption.

George ORWELL, 1984.

1. "Just Do It!"

(How many grams of philosophy in a world of advertising?)

"We're taught that companies are souls, Which is indeed the most terrifying news in the world."
Gilles Deleuze.

Master Yoda said: "No! Don't try. Just do it. Or don't. There is no try."

It was a long time ago, in a galaxy far, far away, when Luke Skywalker was in Jedi training in the Dagobah system, following in the footsteps of his father Anakin, who had turned to the dark side of the Force after becoming Darth Vader. As part of his training program, Luke Skywalker had to lift his X-Wing ship by sheer force of thought: "Master, lifting a stone is one thing... but this is very different." Finally, at his trainer's insistence, Luke complied: "All right, I'll give it a try." What an apprentice phrase! "No! Try not. Do. Or do not. There is no try."

- In English. A long time later, a certain Nike, no doubt heir to a line of ancestors going back to Yoda, adopted the same philosophy: “Just do it!”, rather badly translated into French as “juste fais-le”, but which roughly means: “Just do it (or don’t do it, but there’s no trying).” Incidentally, the meaning of the anglicism “just” has become clearer since Parisians started using it, especially when they’re on TV: “C’était juste énorme!”

Whatever the case, Nike seems to be defending a certain philosophy of life that has nothing to envy the wisdom lessons of Yoda or, closer to home, Socrates. It’s been a long time since advertising simply sold bars of soap. Alfa Romeo uses great phrases to talk about its Giulietta without really talking about it: “Without heart, we’d be nothing but machines - like Darth Vader.” The brand even finds a way to quote Shakespeare: “We are made of the same stuff as dreams” - in relation to *Romeo and Juliet*... It’s beautiful! Another car, the Kia Ceed, has the slogan: “Live intensely.” For its part, BMW announces: “We make more than cars, we create joy”, like Spinoza who, in his main work *Ethics*, also aims to create joy. Fiat doesn’t just build cars either: it’s a “manufacturer of optimism”. Optimism is the philosophy of Leibniz, who asserts that everything is for the best in the “best of all possible worlds”, and which Voltaire mocks in *Candide*. The opposite is pessimism, the philosophy of Arthur Schopenhauer, about which Friedrich Nietzsche wrote extensively. That’s right! I too can come up with great phrases and quotations! Alfa Romeo isn’t the only one who’s done Philo.

Thanks to advertising, we no longer need to inflict ourselves with indigestible pamphlets full of “metaphysical-theological-cosmolonigology": just buy a car and you'll understand everything about life. And if you can't afford one, you can make do with a razor: a Philips TV ad ends with the slogan: "Express yourself every day". Before we get there, the cinematic film shows images of surfers, while a voice-over delivers a speech reminiscent of Martin Luther King's "dream": "We men are all adventurers on the path of discovery. So don't be prisoners of routine, open your eyes, seize every opportunity. Be proud, if by your actions, from the most discreet to the craziest, you have broken the codes". At the end, we learn almost by accident that it was an advert for "Philips shavers and clippers", and we don't see the connection. Especially since it seems hard to "break the codes" by buying the same razor as everyone else, manufactured in millions of copies. So, how many grams of philosophy are there in this world of advertising?

"We are made of the same stuff as dreams". It's probably not for nothing that Alfa Romeo has borrowed this quote from Shakespeare. "The origin of philosophy," said Epictetus, "is the experience we have of our weakness and powerlessness. He was thinking in particular of our weakness in the face of death, as well as our powerlessness to avoid it: we are mortal and there's nothing we can do about it. And when we realize that we're going to die, we can ask ourselves whether life has any meaning: what's the point? It's all the more absurd when it's a 13-year-old dying of leukemia: he's had no time for anything, and the days spent at school preparing for his future will never serve him. I don't think people realize

1. "Just Do It!"

what's in store for them: they probably imagine that they'll die as you fall asleep, only to wake up one day or another. But when we die, it's forever: when do we see each other again? We won't. When I'm dead, I won't remember my parents, my brothers or my children. I won't know that I knew them, that they existed. I won't even remember having existed myself. I'll be nothing to myself, and so I'll be nothing. I'm revolted by this, and my only consolation is to think that you're all going to die too. There is justice! "We're made of the same stuff as dreams, and our little lives are surrounded by sleep." A dream is just an illusion: when you wake up in the morning, you reassure yourself that it was just a dream. It didn't last long, and the return to reality made it disappear. But soon, my life will have been just a dream, because I'll go back to sleep forever, without having lived very long - *lived,* that is, seen, felt and thought things. And when I'm dead, I won't see, feel or think anything. That's cheerful. The question is, why reference all these dark ideas in a slogan for Giulietta? Should it make me want to buy an Alfa Romeo? And above all, what does this have to do with cars?

"Anima Sana In Corpore Sano" (Asics)

With Nike, at least, the philosophical message is not unrelated to the brand's products: since it sells sporting goods, it's not entirely absurd that it should claim to defend the spirit of sport, just like the asics brand whose initials stand for: "Anima Sana In Corpore Sano (A healthy mind in a healthy body)." The name "Nike" itself is not without meaning: in

Greek, the word "*Nikè*" means victory, and in Ancient Greek religion, it was associated with the goddess of war, Athena Nikè, victory - it all comes together, it's just huge!

But why do Nike or Yoda tell us that we shouldn't just try? After all, you can never be sure of anything, and Jean-Paul Sartre himself, in *L'Existentialisme est un humanisme,* reminds us of another great principle: "You don't need to hope to undertake". It's a bit like Luke Skywalker's philosophy: "I'm going to try - without being sure I'll succeed." If we waited until we were sure before taking action, we'd never get anything done. That's how some people tell themselves at election time: my vote's just a drop in the bucket, so there's no point in me voting. Of course, the outcome of an election doesn't just depend on me - it depends on everyone else. But if everyone thought like that, no one would vote. So I have to do what I have to do, without worrying about the result. "All that matters is that I do my civic duty, and then it's up to others to do theirs. As Epictetus, another great Stoic philosopher, said: "There are things that depend on us, and others that don't."

"Just do it!" No questions asked. This is the philosophy defended by the famous Epictetus in his *Manual,* which evokes the case of the athlete: "You want to win at the Olympic Games? Me too, by the gods! But sporting victory, like the result of an election, doesn't depend on you: after all, you can always get hurt, and despite all your efforts, you can come up against someone stronger than you. What counts, once again, is that you've done what you had to do, so you won't regret it. If there's one thing a Nike-sponsored athlete

1. "Just Do It!"

needs to know, it's that you can always lose, and that's what makes victory so beautiful. If I was certain of winning, I'd probably have no joy at all. As Sartre again says: "Success must only be *possible,* that is to say, there is no action unless external difficulties can always be so high or so new that human invention cannot overcome them." Victory must be won *over* something: without a real obstacle to overcome, without a real difficulty to face, there is neither victory nor sport - and the obstacle is only *real* if it makes defeat *possible.*

Yet, if Yoda is to be believed, "Just do it!" could well mean "don't just try", which is pretty much the opposite of everything we've just said. In fact, he's off to a pretty bad start if he starts by saying "I'll try". It's a loser's phrase: what's the point of doing things if you know from the outset that you won't succeed? Voters have to believe that their vote will be used for something, otherwise they wouldn't vote.

In *The Prince,* to illustrate the philosophy of Nike and Yoda - or not - Machiavelli uses the image of archers: "Knowing well the virtue of their bow, they aim much higher than their goal when the latter seems too far away; not to really hit with their arrow at such a great altitude, but to strike, thanks to this high aim, the target they had chosen[1]." As it happens, there are things we can't control, unforeseen events or imponderables, so we never achieve exactly what we set out to do. To hit the target straight ahead, the archer doesn't aim directly

1. MACHIAVELLI, *The Prince,* Chapter VI, translated from the Italian by J. Anglade, Le Livre de Poche, 1983, pages 27-28.

at it, otherwise the arrow would be stuck in the ground long before it arrived. You have to take into account the wind, the arrow's speed, its movement in an arc - in short, everything that means a shot never goes off without a hitch. So, at the start, you have to aim *high*: victory anyway, and with a bit of luck, fourth place. That's what French athletes who often finish at the foot of the podium say: "If someone had told me I'd finish fourth, I'd have signed with both hands." In other words, "I'm disappointed because I was aiming for first place, but in the end, I couldn't have hoped for better." But it was precisely because he was aiming for first place that our French athlete came fourth. Had he been aiming for fourth place, he would probably have finished last. In short, there's a lot of philosophy in a slogan like "Just do it!"

"Coffee is not just black."

Apparently, the philosophy contained in a page of advertising isn't limited to a few grams: it's counted in tons or quintals. And Nike has a lot to do with it. In her excellent *No Logo*, Canadian social-melenchonist activist Naomi Klein believes that the invention of the slogan "Just do it!" constitutes one of the "defining moments of branding[2]". What is *branding*, you may ask? *Branding* is what advertisers think of as philosophy. The term comes from the English word "brand", and "branding" is all the work that goes into building a brand's

2. KLEIN (Naomi), *No Logo*, "Zéro espace", 1, translated from English by M. Saint-Germain, Actes Sud, "J'ai lu essai", 2001, p.46.

1. "Just Do It!"

image. For example, making Nike, which initially sells shoes, come to represent the spirit, even the philosophy, of sport. As Nescafé says of its Dolce Gusto coffee maker: "Coffee is not just black." First of all, you might wonder what's wrong with "just". Secondly, thanks to advertising, we learn not only philosophy, but also foreign languages: all the slogans are in English, all the time. As a result, they're always putting in little stars to translate: "make it happen" (Chevrolet), "move your mind" (Saab), "What else" (Nescafé, again), "may the force be with you" (Yoda), "Luke, I am your father" (Darth Vader), etc., and so on.

"Coffe is not just black" roughly translates as "coffee is not just black", and the phrase sums up the philosophy *of* advertising philosophy quite well. Naomi Klein points out that advertising isn't what it used to be: originally, it consisted of publicizing a product - coffee, a car or sports shoes - by describing the object's characteristics, in the manner of the Opel ads extolling "Deutsche Technologie", the German know-how whose cars include all the functions you'd expect from a car: comfort, safety, performance, etc. If we leave it at that, Nescafé's informative message should be: "Coffee is black!" - and if you'd rather drink something brown, buy yourself some tea. What else is there to say? You could say that coffee is hot. The problem is that all brands have the same products: Asics, Nike or Adidas sell sports shoes, and Nescafé's coffee will always be as black as its competitors'. Faced with the uniformity of consumer products, brands can no longer simply describe the objects they sell, because they are the same. Above all, the companies represented by these brands no longer manufacture anything. As Gilles Deleuze, the favorite philosopher of advertisers, artists and anyone else who doesn't understand philosophy, noted back in 1990: "In the current situation, capitalism is no longer in favor of production, which it often relegates to the periphery of the Third World (...): it buys ready-made products, or assembles spare parts[3]." If Nike can't really boast of its know-how or the quality of its manufacturing, it's because the company doesn't manufacture any shoes, or anything it sells: it buys its products itself from Chinese or Indonesian factories *in the Third World,* which, incidentally, manufacture the same shoes for other brands. So, if Nike doesn't make sports goods, what does it make? What is Nike?

Well, Nike makes Nike. The company, and all those it employs, work solely to build the brand's image, using *values* and *concepts.* Neither Nescafé nor Nike produce anything concrete, nor any of the material objects they sell, since these are manufactured by others: they produce these completely abstract things called "concepts"[4]. A concept is really just

3. DELEUZE (Gilles), *Pourparlers (1972-1990),* V, 17, Les Éditions de Minuit, "Reprise", 2003, page 245.

4. Facebook's IPO on May 18, 2012 symbolizes the abstract nature of brands: Facebook sells nothing, produces nothing, apart from ad-funded web pages. Mark Zuckerberg, Facebook's founder, represents the "capitalist" as Deleuze presented him back in 1990: "What he wants to sell are services, and what he wants to buy are shares" (*Pour parlers, 1972-1990,* V, 17, *op. cit,* page 245.) Except that the operation was a fiasco: the company was apparently overvalued. Finally, there are limits to what you can sell.

1. "Just Do It!"

an idea, or at least a word that designates an idea. There are rather concrete words like *coffee* or *car*, which correspond to material objects that everyone can see and touch: I can put my coffee in front of me, on the table. But there are other words that refer to ideas that exist only in our minds. Happiness, freedom, justice, good or evil are concepts. You understand that justice is not something you can put on a table: what would it look like? A man can act justly, but justice itself cannot be seen: it's a view of the mind. Justice is our idea of what is right. So what is just? What is justice? Perhaps it's the role of philosophy to answer these questions and "create concepts"[5], like Plato in his dialogues, which each time seek to define an idea: in *The Banquet*, love; in The *Crito*, duty; and in *The Meno*, virtue. And Nike? Doesn't Nike also create concepts by coming up with the slogan "Just do it"? After all, it's the answer to the question: what is sport? Which is no mean feat.

One day, while shopping with my girlfriend, we entered a Zadig & Voltaire boutique (Frédéric Lefebvre's favorite book). She came across a pretty pair of multicolored mittens and said to me:

"What do you think?

- Did you see the price? I reply. 75 euros! That's 500 francs! All that for gloves with fingers missing!

- Yes, but they're Zadig & Voltaire!"

---

5. Deleuze (Gilles), *Pourparlers (1972-1990)*, IV, 13, *op. cit.*, page 186.

"Today," noted Deleuze, "it's information technology, communication and commercial promotion that are appropriating the words *concept* and *creative*[6]." When Nescafé declares: "Coffee is not just black", it is to assert the philosophical role of advertising. "Coffee is not just black" means that our coffee isn't just coffee - it's drinkable, and that's that. In the Nescafé brand, there's much more than coffee: a lifestyle, values, or even George Clooney - *what else?* And in a Nike shoe, there's much more than laces: there's a sporting spirit, and all the values that the designers have managed to associate with the brand. Consumers don't buy material objects, and what distinguishes brands is not their products - which are all the same. It's their image, or rather, their philosophy, through which customers assert their way of being and thinking.

Throughout his trial, the "East Paris killer" Guy Georges wore a Umbro sweatshirt. Guy Georges sported an *Umbro* sweatshirt. Shortly afterwards, I got the impression that everyone was buying the same brand of clothes, because it was classy to have the same sweater as a serial killer. You can't always completely control your image and values. But what can we say? "Some things depend on us, and others don't."

6. *Ibid.*

1. "Just Do It!"

"Whatever you do, do it carefully without losing sight of the end."

On a goose-poop TV set reminiscent of *Apostrophe*, a pedantic young nerd chats with other pedantic nerds. It's an advert for the Citroën DS4 "mat". Apparently, the speaker has written a book, the cover of which appears behind him: *Clepsydre*. First of all, the title makes no sense. What's more, the pseudo-writer listens to himself talking, quoting Aristotle or something, with incomprehensible sentences and Latin words: "Whatever you do, do it with prudence without losing sight of the end, *quid quid agis prudenter agas et respice finem*. This Pythagorean system allows us to infer a generic function from the notion of determinism: we can gravitate, we can transmute..." At the end, the slogan "shine differently" appears on a black background to cut off the nerd, a way of saying: "*Shut up.*" So there you have it: for advertising and those who watch it, that's what philosophy is all about: words that mean nothing and that nobody understands. And in the DS4 ad, the phrases actually mean nothing - don't worry. So it's easy to see why adverts are sometimes content to use big phrases that sound philosophical, *just* because they sound good, without us really knowing what they mean.

"We're made of the same stuff as dreams", or "nothing is more stable than change". How philosophical! It's Alfa Romeo all over again. They must have been happy after their "*Skype conf*" brainstorming session, when they came up with this, and no doubt the *creative* who stumbled across this phrase while sorting out his college courses was proud of himself: “Hey, guys! What do you think? Isn’t this sentence huge?!” It brings to mind the Greek philosopher Heraclitus, who said: “You can’t enter the same river twice[7].” Or how about Nietzsche: “What doesn’t kill me makes me stronger”, or Oscar Wilde: “The best way to resist temptation is to give in to it”, even if that’s the kind of quote every high-school girl puts on her Facebook profile. Still, it’s philosophical! So much so that a certain Dominique Quessada, an advertising executive (who believes himself to be) reconverted to philosophy, writes: “Despite the scandal it represents for thought, advertising constitutes the triumph and completion of philosophy.” And that’s all there is to it.

To philosophize is to learn how to live, and advertising slogans teach us how to live: “Express yourself”, “Shine differently”, “Drink. Eliminate.” Advertising seems to speak like a philosopher. Epicurus used to say, “The recommendations I continually address to you, put them into practice and make them the object of your care, recognizing in them distinctly the elements of the good life.”[8] In fact, according to the famous Dominique Quessada, advertising has the same purpose as philosophy: to explain to men how to live in order to be happy. According to Epicurus, “We must

7. Quoted by Plutarch, *in* DUMONT (J.-P.) *Les présocratiques*, “Héraclite”, Gallimard, “Bibliothèque de la Pléiade”, 1988, page 167.
8. EPICURUS, *Lettre à Ménécée*, translated from the Greek by P.-M. Morel, GF-Flammarion, “Édition avec dossier”, 2009, page 44.

1. “Just Do It!”

therefore devote our care to that which produces happiness". In its advert for the aptly named Mito, Alfa Romeo offers yet another lesson in life:

"One day, it's a realization, like a big slap in the face. You're different, you decide to finally be yourself, to do only what makes you tick, what makes you come alive. You're all adrenaline, there's no stopping you. It's like a new road that keeps opening up in front of you, because... nothing is more stable than change." Basically, the style isn't too far removed from Aristotle's faux phrase in the DS4 ad: "Whatever you do, do it carefully without losing sight of the end." Except that advertising is much better than philosophy, because at least we understand what it's saying. At the same time, Alfa Romeo's philosophy is a lot like Philips' famous speech: "Don't be a prisoner of routine, seize every opportunity, break the codes, etc." So, not only are the brands all the same, but so is their café du commerce philosophy. And then there's Jeep Wrangler, with its little adventurous film: "It's when you follow your own path that you feel truly alive." How original! But when it comes to philosophy, we seem to be hearing the same banalities over and over again.

"Shine differently."

Some commercials are memorable and unforgettable. I remember the ones from the 80s because of the music: the Heineken or Kronenbourg beer ads in the cinema, with Robert Palmer's "Every kind of people" or Elton John's "Song for guy" on the piano. The grain of the image, the sun setting on the beach and, above all, the music, created an atmosphere that I've never found elsewhere, and for which I'm still nostalgic. Like the Wollmark ad, I think, with a slow song that broke my heart: "change your heart, look around you... Everybody's got to learn sometimes". I also remember Pacific, "force Anis", with the girl getting out of the water by leaving her footprint on wooden planks. And my favorite "all over the world" is the Fahrenheit ad, with the guy walking through the desert, before ending up at the end of a jetty, facing the sea. Once again, a very cinematic image grain and atmosphere that have nothing to envy the staging of the best films. There's no doubt that the designer himself imagines himself to be making art, or even philosophy, when he finds phrases like: "you decide to finally be you, to do only what makes you vibrate, what makes you come alive". Since Nike, "the advertiser has ceased to see himself as a huckster and has become 'the philosopher-king of commercial culture'[9]". And if it's so hard to see the connection between the Philips razor and the advertising that goes with it, it's because there really is no connection. The shoes and cars for sale are merely pretexts for guiding lost sheep along the path of life, giving moral lessons, transmitting political messages, or even producing genuine works of art. So, is the advertising executive the modern-day artist or philosopher?

You only have to look at this DS4 ad to understand what advertisers think of the philosopher: a clown who quotes

9. KLEIN (Naomi), *op. cit.* page 31.

1. "Just Do It!"

Aristotle to shine in society. It's like in the famous *Allegory of the Cave,* where Plato tells us that men laugh at the philosopher who comes to give them lessons: "Wouldn't he be a laughing stock, and we'd say about him that having gone up there he came back with his sight spoiled, and that it wasn't worth it"? "Brillez autrement" ("Shine differently"), a play on words with the DS4 "just mat", whose paintwork doesn't shine, and even "flambant neuf" ("brand new"), it doesn't flare. That's what advertising philosophy is all about: if we talk, it's to shine in society. It's not what you say that counts, it's the effect you have on others, and if possible, the most beautiful effect. But is the purpose of a car to shine? Funny philosophy, funny *life lesson.* But who cares? It's what the consumer believes, what he's looking for when he buys a car. So we give them what they want, and tell them what they want to hear.

In his *Allegory of the Cave,* Plato imagines men trapped in a cave since childhood, chained from head to toe. They've never been out of the cave, so they don't know that there's a world outside. They are also unaware that behind their backs there are other men, "puppet-showmen" who manipulate "all sorts of manufactured objects", wooden horses, dolls and other "puppets". And thanks to the light of a fire, the shadows of the puppets are projected onto the rock face of the cave. But the prisoners see neither the fire nor the puppeteers behind them, like a projectionist behind the audience in a movie theater. All they see are the shadows of the puppets on the wall in front of them. In short, the prisoners are in a state of illusion: they've only ever seen shadows, and don't know that these are just silhouettes. They've never seen the puppeteers, and don't know they're being manipulated. For Plato, these prisoners are us, the human beings, and the puppeteers are all the *smooth-talkers* who manipulate us and lull us into delusion, the better to keep us prisoners. At the time, Plato was certainly referring to religion, which promises eternal life and tells us how to live and think, in the name of a God no one has ever seen: "love thy neighbor as thyself", don't do this, don't do that, and so on. Plato also points to the politicians who promise us the fourThursday week in order to get elected and stay in power. Above all, he's thinking of the famous sophists like Protagoras, the *communication* advisors of the time, whom the sons of good families paid dearly to make a success of their political careers by bamboozling idiots. The art of sophists or communication advisors is rhetoric, the power of *persuasion*. But today, those who tell us what to do are no longer the religious, nor the politicians, since we no longer believe in them. So, aren't these *puppeteers* even more into advertising? Today, that's where they tell us how we should live, and what we should think.

Wiiilliam Saurin! (different communication techniques)

It's true that the music of Heineken or Kronenbourg ads sticks in your head. It's a whole era, like that other Robert Palmer song for the 205, "Johnny and Mary": cars for living. The music in the Mercedes ad is also brilliant, and quite reminiscent of the soundtrack to the film *Drive*. By the

1. "Just Do It!"

way, it's the same composer: a certain Kavinsky. So it's not Mercedes, it's Kavinsky. You can always create a brand image and even a mood by using music. Advertising always works the same way: we're lulled into a sense of hipness, freshness and freedom, to the sound of folk guitars. Music is practical: it's artistic expression that immediately plunges us into an emotional state. It makes us experience a whole range of feelings immediately and quite artificially. Advertising gives us the impression of rediscovering the *cathartic* effects which, according to Aristotle, characterize works of art such as films and music, which make us laugh and cry. Doesn't advertising music also make us feel these kinds of emotions? And aren't those humorous ads we play over and over again on "publivores' night" funny? There's also a lot of humor in advertising, a kind of *second degree* where consumer society pokes fun at itself, with those hilarious puns like: "Monfort, c'est mon faible" or "Il n'y a que Maille qui m'aille". Amusing, isn't it?

But behind the humor of the ads, there's always the same goal: to give a good brand image, to sell. And behind the halo of the most moving musical flights of fancy, there's never more than a telephone subscription, a car or a yoghurt. The role of music is to make material objects seem like great spiritual experiences. Is advertising trying to get us out of the cave? No. The aim is rather to get a message into our heads, like digging a little deeper into the walls of the cave with a sledgehammer. As in those William Saurin ads that take up the Village People's "YMCA" melody: "Wiiilliam Saurin! Wiiilliam Saurin! Your poulet basquaise, your blanquette de veau, your boeuf bourguignon..." It's not very fancy, but it's very effective. And at least we don't pretend to make tin cans sound like philosophers.

Creating concepts, yes, but for what? In the *Allegory of the Cave*, Plato presents the philosopher as the one who frees the prisoners, undoes their chains and leads them outside. Then they discover that they've been deluded and wrong all along. This means that philosophy leads us to question the opinions to which we have always been *attached*. For example, it may be difficult to be happy knowing that we're going to die, because we wonder whether life has any meaning. The philosopher teaches us to live with this idea. "Get used to the fact that death is nothing to us," says Epicurus. We shouldn't be afraid of death, because we won't feel anything anymore. In the meantime, as long as we feel something, we should enjoy the pleasures of life, whether long or short: the wise man "does not seek (...) to enjoy the longest moment, but the most pleasant". Does advertising teach us to question our fears, beliefs and opinions? Let's just say it prefers to sell us credit, insurance and creams to keep us young. Instead of curing us of our fears, she maintains them and uses them. It rides the wave and pushes us ever deeper into the cave, telling us what we want to hear, because the aim is always the same: to push the consumer to buy. The DS4 "matte" promises to "shine in a different way": but should we try to shine, especially when we have a beautiful car? Oenobiol promises to lose weight and 4 cm of waistline per month *just* by swallowing pills before going to bed. Let's face it. But

1. "Just Do It!"

why do we absolutely have to lose weight? To fit in with the advertised canons of beauty? Afterwards, we can always be asked to *break the codes*.

It's hard to imagine Epicurus or Socrates footnoting their books to warn us that "everything I've just said is wrong". And yet, that's exactly what we see in the ads: yoghurts and cakes, sweets and chocolates encourage us to indulge freely. In the horrifying *Nutella* ads, we're told about all the good things in the spread, the *good* milk, the *good* chocolate - obviously, we're not going to say it's bad - before concluding, "It takes energy to be a kid." And then, in a small banner at the bottom of the screen, we read: "Avoid eating too much fat, too much sugar." This message is a bit like the daylight we see at the bottom of the cave, reminding us that everything is wrong. Like the little "out" light above the cinema door, which prevents us from being completely "in the movie".

A famous 1980s ad said, "Canada Dry, it looks like alcohol, it's golden like alcohol, but it's not alcohol." Advertising is the Canada Dry of philosophy.

2. "That's the game, my poor Lucette!"

(What is happiness?)

"We perish by the example of others.
We'll heal for a little
that we separate ourselves from the crowd."
SENECA.

"Happiness is as simple as a phone call."

"Living happily", wrote Seneca, "is what all men want, but as for discerning what makes life happy, they are in the dark. And it's so hard to achieve the happy life[10]". Apparently, this so-called Stoic *philosopher* never ate Saint-Albray cheese: he would have known that "the best things in life are the simplest".

And since the invention of the telephone, we also know that "happiness is as simple as a phone call". But in Seneca's day, there were no telephones. So he couldn't have known that.

10. SÉNÈQUE, *La vie heureuse*, première partie, I.1. translated from the Latin by Pierre Pellegrin, *in* SÉNÈQUE, *La vie heureuse, la Brièveté de la vie*, GF-Flammarion, 2005, page 45.

Today, thanks to advertising, everyone knows what makes people happy: cheese, a telephone and, for the fussiest, an MMA policy, because "happiness is guaranteed". But to afford all this, you need money, and the easiest way is to win the lottery. Everyone knows that too - except Seneca.

We don't force people to play Loto, yet they play anyway. So they must know why. Of course, they're not idiots: they don't believe they have much chance of winning. What they do believe, however, is that they'll be happy if they win millions - and in the meantime, they feel unhappy that they don't have them yet. But what do they really know? In one of its advertisements, La Française des Jeux itself warns us: "And you, what will you do when you've won?" In fact, you'd do well to ask yourself that very question. As Seneca said: "We must first establish what it is we are to seek"[11]. Before spending a fortune playing the lottery, we should first ask ourselves what would make us happy. Is it something that can be bought? But we don't ask ourselves this question, and the Française des Jeux simply reiterates what everyone thinks they know: in these ads, the hypothetical winners end up in a villa with a swimming pool or on a beach with coconut palms. In short, it's easy to *discern* what makes people happy: money, material goods (cell phone, 3D screen, car, villa with pool, etc.) and a heavenly location "under the sun".

For those who still have doubts, La Française des Jeux has come up with *the* killer ad: "C'est le jeu ma pauvre Lucette!"

11. *Ibid.*

But what game? As the TV advert shows, you have to spin a globe to let chance decide your next travel destination. The result?

"Australia!

- Again?!

- That's the game, my poor Lucette."

So this is what *we're supposed to be looking for*, this is what you're supposed to do when you've won the Lotto: travel. Where to? Anywhere. Oddly enough, the world map doesn't stop at Iraq, or worse, Melun. No, it's *Australia*. Because it's so far away, it must be very expensive. That said, if Lucette lets chance decide for her, it's because she hasn't quite *worked out what she's* looking for: she doesn't know what she wants, or where she wants to go. And it doesn't really matter. Unlike Seneca, the ad argues that it's pointless to start by *establishing what we should be looking for* and knowing what we want. Sure, it may be hard to know what makes you happy, but whatever it is, money will get it. So we have to start by having money. A bank card advertisement claims, "There are some things you can't buy." But nobody believes it. Even before we've really asked ourselves what we want, we think it's something that can be bought. Lucette is disappointed when she learns that it will be Australia: "Again?! But it doesn't matter: if she doesn't want to go to Australia anymore, she can always choose another destination. And even if she doesn't want to travel at all, she'll be able to afford everything. There's no other way to be happy. Money allows you to satisfy all your desires and even, as the sophist

2. "That's the game, my poor Lucette!"

Callicles put it, "to fill all your desires as they blossom[12]". There's no need to know in advance what I want: thanks to money, the world will adapt to my desires.

In any case, Lucette is under no obligation to go anywhere: it's just a game, a purely free activity with no real purpose. When we play, it's always for no reason, simply because we feel like it, and it's always *for the fun of it*, as they say: the only aim is to please ourselves. Usually - when you're poor - you don't really have time to play, because you have to work. And work is just about the opposite of play: you don't work for no reason, and certainly not for pleasure, but because you have to. And you don't work for nothing, but to earn money to meet your needs and satisfy your desires. So, when you already have money, what do you do? You do what Lucette did: you have nothing left but free time and leisure. Lucette's game tells us that happiness consists in not working. In the famous Loto ads, the winner disguises himself as a chick to tell his employer: "Au revoir! Au revoir! President!" The implication is that work is nothing but constraint, suffering and humiliation. In short, it's what makes us unhappy[13].

At the same time, if you look closely at the ad, you can tell that Lucette and her husband are retired: you can tell by their old-fashioned voices and the famous first name

12. Plato, *Gorgias*, 491 d-492c, *in* Plato, *Protagoras, Euthydemus, Gorgias, Menexenus, Menon, Cratylus*, GF-Flammarion, 1993, page 235.

13. Yet another ad shows a man who has failed at everything he's tried to do, such as setting up an amusement park. No need to work, then: the only way to earn money is to play the Lotto.

"Lucette", which probably hasn't been given to a newborn since 1940. You can also tell by the tacky interior decoration and the old-fashioned furniture that smells of mothballs. After all, Lucette had already stopped working before she won the Lotto. So she had time on her hands. But with no money, she was condemned to boredom in her old man's living room, waiting to die. Now she has everything she needs to be happy: free time and the money to fill it. But then, if Lucette has everything to be happy, why take this blasé tone? How can she still be disappointed when her husband tells her it's Australia?

- Again!?

"Hurlez de plaisir" (pleasure, joy and happiness)

"Fleury Michon. Ain't life grand?" Why not? Because I eat ham? Well, it depends: I'd have a hard time consoling myself with my ham if I made myself a sandwich because I had nothing else to eat, given that I've been sleeping under a bridge since I lost my job and my wife left me. Ah yes, but no! It works if you're in your country house with your family or friends, if the weather's nice, if you've got a job and everything. So, what's ham got to do with it? Once you've stripped away everything else and are left with a slice of ham, what's life really like?

Needless to say, advertisements try to sell us products, and the most hackneyed slogan - so hackneyed that nobody believes it anymore - is that these goods will make us happy. Happiness would be simple to define, reduced to a single

2. "That's the game, my poor Lucette!"

thing: a slice of ham, an insurance policy or a bottle of soda - "open Coca-Cola, open happiness". And this happiness would be just as easy to obtain, since all you'd have to do is buy it. But it's not so simple to *discern* what makes life happy or *beautiful*.

The dictionary defines happiness as "a state of fully satisfied consciousness". And in the same vein, Kant speaks of "the satisfaction of all our inclinations[14]". But what does it mean to be "fully satisfied"? After buying shoes, we might say to ourselves: "I've found my happiness. But just because a pair of shoes makes you happy doesn't mean you're "fully satisfied". In fact, there are several degrees of satisfaction: we can be *happy*, which is a minimum - we're *satisfied with* very little. Above that, there's undoubtedly pleasure, then joy, and so on. One imagines that finding a job after two years of unemployment gives rise to much stronger feelings than a pair of shoes - contrary to what the hysterical cries of the buyers in the ads for the Zalando.fr online sales site suggest. And happiness would be the ultimate, or as Kant put it a little better, "a maximum of well-being", a pleasure such as no other exists.

In short, when you're happy, you're *fulfilled*. When you*'re happy*, you don't need or lack anything. In a sense, happiness consists in no longer desiring anything. But can a pair of shoes, a slice of ham or a piece of cheese really fill the void

14. KANT, *Critique of Pure Reason*, II, chapter II, second section, translated from the German by A. Tremesaygues and B. Pacaud. Pacaud, PUF, "Quadrige", 1990, page 544.

of my desires? It's doubtful. First of all, these little pleasures don't overwhelm us to the point of compensating for all the dissatisfactions we might otherwise experience: a cheese doesn't make us forget unemployment. Here again, Zalando.fr ads are misleading - obviously[15]. But if a new pair of shoes can't make us *fully satisfied, it's* mainly because the pleasure won't last. One day, maybe tomorrow, we'll feel the need to buy another. And yet, if we were truly satisfied, we'd want for nothing, neither today nor tomorrow. "The idea of happiness", writes Kant, suggests "an absolute whole, a maximum of well-being in my present state and in any state that might be mine in the future"[16]. So, what can make us so happy?

"Bon Zapetti" (unattainable happiness)

Certainly not ham. As we've seen, you'd also have to have a house, a family, a job, sun, health *and everything*. And *everything* what? That's the problem: we don't really know where to stop. As President would say, "eating well is the beginning of happiness", but where is the end? Is there even one? Could we make a list of everything that makes us happy? We can only guess that something will always be missing, and that it seems impossible to have *everything you* need to be happy.

15. Another TV ad features a bank robbery Everyone has to lie on the floor, but the "hostage" women start talking about their purchases on Zalando.fr. When a delivery man bursts into the bank - who knows why - the girls rush to him, waxing, and forget all about the bank robbers.
16. KANT, *Foundations of the Metaphysics of Morals*, Second Section, translated from the German by Victor Delbos, Delagrave, 1985, page 131.

2. "That's the game, my poor Lucette!"

Take Lucette, who learns that she'll have to go to Australia *again*: her weariness, her very disappointment, is supposed to show us that she's found happiness. Strange: why should her dissatisfaction show us that she's *fully satisfied*? It's obvious: thanks to Lotto money, it's so "easy to achieve happiness" that we don't even realize how lucky we are. While so many others lament the fact that they can't travel, Lucette no longer even feels the desire to do so - "yet?" So she no longer lacks anything, at least on that front - that's that! And what appears to others as an unattainable *dream* has become Lucette's daily routine, a habit she can even afford to refuse[17].

But isn't *poor Lucette* showing us that happiness is completely unattainable? If she were truly fulfilled, she should be "happy to contemplate what she possesses, without ever interrupting this joy"[18]. Happy to contemplate her money, happy to go to Australia again. Instead, Lucette

17. In a similar vein, an Internet advert for the SNCF (French national railways) touts the merits of low-price TGV tickets, up to 50% off: in the picture, a girl has apparently just returned from vacation. She's so tanned that she still has the marks of her sunglasses and swimsuit. She's in the bathroom with her husband, who's brushing his teeth and says, "Stéphane, are we going on vacation again? I think I look pale." Ah! Ah! In fact, she's not pale at all: but thanks to cheap TGV tickets, it's so easy to go on vacation so often that two days without a tan already seems like an eternity. The question is, is being tanned really happiness? In his excellent *bonheur conforme* qu'il est difficile de dépasser, François Brune begins by writing: "false happiness with a tan remains the most debilitating of the ills of modern existence." BRUNE (François), *Le bonheur conforme*, Gallimard, "Le monde actuel", 1985, page 9).

18. SÉNÈQUE, *De la tranquillité de l'âme*, II, 4, in SÉNÈQUE, *De la providence, De la constance du sage, De la tranquillité de l'âme, Du loisir*, translated from Latin by P. Miscevic, GF-Flammarion, 2002, page 134.

finds a way to lament, like everyone else who still hasn't won the Lotto. In fact, maybe nothing can ever satisfy us, because we get tired of everything. And Lucette is like everyone else: her umpteenth trip to Australia no longer makes her jump for joy. What we call happiness in the strict sense," writes Freud, "results from the rather *sudden* satisfaction of accumulated needs[19]." *Sudden*: only the ephemeral moment when we get what we didn't have is a source of pleasure or joy. Similarly, you need to have an appetite to enjoy eating. In fact, we usually wish each other *bon appétit!* But what's good about appetite? It's hunger, a feeling of lack. And those who can't eat when they're hungry, those who can't find the means to satisfy this need, must certainly suffer, all the more so if their situation is set to last. When we think of *world hunger,* we think of misery and suffering. And yet, what pleasure is there in eating when you're not hungry? There isn't. It's more like having *your back teeth knocked out*. It's out of lack, need or desire, then, that pleasure and the famous *happiness that* can be found in a trip or a new pair of shoes. It's all there: it has to be new or *sudden.* Lucette doesn't want to go back to Australia: she wants to discover a place she hasn't been *before* - even Melun.

Shortly after eating, hunger strikes again. We never eat once and for all. As Freud says again in *Le malaise dans la civilisation,* "we can enjoy intensely only contrast, and very

19. Freud, *Le malaise dans la civilisation*, II, translated from the German by B. Lortholary, Éditions Points, page 63.

2. "That's the game, my poor Lucette!"

little of a state[20]." For example, it's often said that the most important thing is to be healthy. But who gets pleasure, even joy, from being healthy? No one does. Because you don't feel anything when you're healthy: you don't feel your liver, your kidneys or your intestines. The only time you're happy to be healthy is when you're coming out of an illness: happy not to suffer from your bowels, happy not to be bedridden. But when you've been healthy for too long, you don't even realize it, and you don't get any pleasure from it.

"That's the game, my poor Lucette!" To experience any joy, you need a little suffering. So we can never be happy, because we're incapable of experiencing lasting pleasure. It's our nature, and there's nothing we can do about it. Otherwise, why keep saying "my poor Lucette", when she's so rich?

Family man (indefinable happiness)

Far from being as simple as a phone call, happiness may be imaginary. As Kant says, "Happiness is an ideal, not of reason, but of the imagination[21]". First of all, an ideal is never just an idea, in the sense that it doesn't exist in reality - you just have ideas. And if it's not real, it's simply because it's impossible: the ideal evokes perfection, and suggests that it's not of this world. *The ideal would be that...*, but that's not possible. After that, we can at least think of *an ideal of reason*: even if it doesn't exist, we know precisely what we'd

20. *Ibid*, page 64.
21. KANT, *Foundations of the Metaphysics of Morals, op. cit.*, page 132.

like, and therefore we know what we have to do to get it. For example, we might want no more children in the world to die of hunger. We know we'll never get there completely, but we can try to get as close as possible. On the other hand, an ideal *of the imagination* is all the less achievable because we don't even know what we're talking about, or what we're thinking of: "despite every man's desire to achieve happiness, no one can ever say in precise terms [...] what he really wants and desires[22]."

In fact, we wouldn't be able to answer the famous question: "What are you going to do when you've won? It's easy to imagine that the millions won in the Lotto will enable you to buy anything you want. Or rather, we don't imagine it well enough, because we don't know what we want. We just tell ourselves that the object that would fill us with happiness must be very valuable, and we deduce that it must be expensive. But we probably confuse price with value, as the other guy would say[23]. When it comes to defining *in precise terms* the object that would make us happy, we can't think of anything in particular[24].

---

22. *Ibid*, page 131.
23. WILDE (Oscar), *The Picture of Dorian Gray*, chapter IV.
24. "Volvo 850: there are only two things in the world capable of making a human being fully happy. This is the second. What's the first? Of course, it's the famous *ideal of imagination that everyone* would like to find without even knowing what they're looking for. So it's obviously ridiculous to claim that a car will do just as well. But it's especially optimistic, or delusional, to claim that there are at least "two things in the world" that can make us "fully satisfied". Is there only one?

2. "That's the game, my poor Lucette!"

Perhaps a kind of Grail or philosopher's stone that everyone would like to find without even knowing what they're looking for. But is it something that can be bought? Is it even something as specific as a material object? That would be astonishing, given that happiness is far too big to fit inside a Coca-Cola bottle - which is not the case for carcinogenic dyes.

Since we don't know what we're looking for, we can never really be sure that we've found it. Even if I'm happy with my situation, if I feel pleasure or even joy in driving this car, living in this house or with this family, I can't really know if I've reached "maximum well-being". I feel satisfied, but am I "fully satisfied"? Who's to say I wouldn't be even happier with another car, another job, another family - in short, another life? Is this really the life I've been looking for? To realize that, I'd have to have had a glimpse of the rest. In fact, that's what *Family Man,* a little American comedy starring Nicholas Cage, shows: a student leaves his college girlfriend to study in London. He never sees her again and becomes a super-rich businessman, which allows him to multiply his female conquests. In short, a certain idea of success. And then, as so often happens in these comedies, a spell from who knows where throws him back into the life he would have had if he'd chosen to stay with the girl from the beginning rather than move to London. And what had to happen happened: he discovers that, in fact, life as a suburban family man with a crummy job is a hell of a lot better. For what it's worth. In any case, we see that happiness can be an illusion, or at least that we can always be happier than we think. But to know that, you'd have to experience other lives. Just as you'd have to wake up to realize that you'd been dreaming.

Finally, since we can never be sure of having achieved happiness, we always tell ourselves that there must be something better out there, so we're unable to be satisfied with anything. We're always afraid we've missed out on something, even if we don't know it. The tragedy, then, is that the pursuit of happiness prevents us from being happy: knowing whether we're fully satisfied is an infinite, even impossible quest. We'll always suspect that there's something better out there, and so we'll always desire what we don't have, without ever being able to be content with what we do have. And of course, advertising claims to put an end to this search for the *absolute everything* or *maximum well-being*, like SFR, which promises "Absolute unlimited. Les illimythics." A telephone subscription is the Holy Grail. Happiness is as easy as a phone call. But if I get a call with bad news, will I be happy?

"I want it all!"

"Those who want everything want TPS." Really? I was thinking more of a job that would allow me to *realize* myself, as they say, and even, I confess, a literary work that would allow me to be recognized. I wanted to be an artist. Maybe because I like to seduce. As many conquests in love as possible, to satisfy all my inclinations, I'm ashamed to say, but that's what I'd like. Besides, as far back as I can remember, I've always wanted to live in New York: it's my consumer

2. "That's the game, my poor Lucette!"

side, no doubt, too influenced by the TV that fills us with American culture. But still: New York! A shack in the South, too, like everyone else. I imagine waking up in the morning in my mas provençal, having breakfast on the terrace, in the sun - with my friend Ricoré. A cliché, but a good one. In fact, I think I'm afraid of dying, and that everything I do, deep down, is explained by a desire for immortality.

- No, no: you're wrong: those who want it all want TPS. *You* want TPS. When it comes to immortality, travel, the life of an artist and Dom Juan, you need a satellite subscription so you can watch all the TV channels, even Téléshopping. Isn't that nice? This is what you want!

Advertising claims to know me better than I do, and to be able to answer that famous question so difficult for Seneca and Kant: what do I really want? Secondly, it holds out the mirage of that elusive *whole* that would make us fully satisfied: the totality of the yet unlimited series of objects we would need if we were to want for nothing. Kant wrote that "happiness is the satisfaction of all our inclinations", in other words, of all our desires. Indeed, if I have a penchant for alcohol or for someone else, it's because my feelings, my nature, in short, something in me draws me towards the drink or this person, so that I experience pleasure or at least satisfaction when I drink - or when I'm with them. But to satisfy all my inclinations, I'd have to know what they are. "First of all, we have to be clear about what is the object of our desire. What am I inclined towards? Do I even know myself well enough to know? I may be mistaken in believing that the life of a businessman or CFO would suit me, that it would correspond to my desires, my aspirations, even my vocation. I can believe I've satisfied my inclinations - for money, for professional success - and then realize that, deep down, I'm more suited to a family life in which I'd feel happier. The businessman's blues. What do I know? Fortunately, there's Findus.

But who can believe that everything that makes you happy can be found in a subscription to satellite or telephone channels? As if *everything* meant "all TV channels"[25]. This is obviously reductive. Happiness doesn't refer to a totality of things or objects, but rather to the totality of our desires or *inclinations* that seem impossible to satisfy. Pleasure never lasts, and desire is always reborn: a new pair of shoes, another trip, somewhere other than Australia. Besides, one person's happiness is probably not the same as another's, and if it's so difficult to know what makes someone happy, it's because nobody wants the same thing. We don't have the same inclinations, and each of us must have our own idea of happiness. So how can we pretend to think for others?

25. In the same vein, the Lesieur "Isio 4" ad serves up a song: "I want it all." So "everything" what? "I want it all: four good associated oils to take care of our health. I want it all: I want something new, vitamin D formula. I want it all." Same reduction of "everything" to not much.

2. "That's the game, my poor Lucette!"

"If you don't have an iPhone, you don't have an iPhone."

Everyone has their own idea of happiness? So why do we keep coming back to the same images: love, money, a villa or a vacation in the sun? If we stopped following clichés and looked for happiness, we might have a better chance of finding it. Where do most of my desires come from, and these famous *inclinations that* are supposed to be mine? I've never owned an iPhone, I've never seen Australia, and yet I think I know I should miss it. As our very own Seneca remarks, "nothing entangles us in greater evils than to regulate ourselves according to the rumors that run about, in the idea that the best is what is generally received, and it is to live not according to reason, but by imitation[26] ". We don't want what we lack, but what others have, without knowing if it would make us happy too, and without even knowing if they themselves are really happy. But it doesn't matter! Whatever I have - a Doucoeur family, a *good* job or lots of money - all that matters is that others envy me. And what makes me happy is *the image* I reflect back to them. That's why I try to conform to the clichés of happiness: who would know that I've made a success of my life if my happiness didn't correspond to the idea that others have of it?

In fact, our *desires* come from what surrounds us. And advertising has understood this. It is undoubtedly no stranger to the existence of these clichés in which we believe we can find what *we should be looking for*. "Conforming happiness",

26. SENECA, *The Happy Life, op. cit,* I, 2, page 46.

as François Brune calls it[27], is all the more mediocre as it is reduced to commodities, or at least, *consumable goods* that we simply have to buy. Is it really reasonable to believe that life will be good with ham? And it's all the more deceptive in that, on the pretext of satisfying our desires, advertising seeks to make us dissatisfied and unhappy, otherwise it couldn't sell us anything.

"If you don't have an iPhone, you don't have an iPhone". That's how the ad ends, after showing us all the applications available on the device. A way of saying that you've really missed out on life. Advertising is the perpetual *Family Man*: showing people what they've missed, what they don't have, trying to make them understand that they should miss it. In case you were happy, *I'd ask you to stop*. In fact, advertising sells us happiness, it claims to show us better than anyone else what the path to happiness is, but it works to make us unhappy, to create desire where none existed before. Do I really have to be unhappy because I have an iPhone 3G and not an iPhone 4G? What difference does it make? What am I *missing*? In fact, it would be better to take their famous slogan literally: "if you don't have an iPhone, you don't have an iPhone", and that's that. It's just a phone. You've got the rest. Coming across a happy man is the worst thing that can happen to an advertiser: you won't sell anything to someone who really knows how to be content with what they've got.

27. BRUNE (François), *Le bonheur conforme, op. cit.* 1985.

2. "That's the game, my poor Lucette!"

Of the tranquility of the soul

"That's the game, my poor Lucette!" But why should we have to go to the other side of the world to be happy? Oh! Not to live there! No, traveling far away is a bit like the pilgrimage to Mecca: you have to have been there at least once, otherwise you've really missed out on life. But why do commercials spend so much time selling us on the idea of "somewhere else"?

I remember seeing posters in the metro for an online travel agency with discounted airfares - another one! The image shows people sticking their heads in the hole of a fake set. You know, the kind of game you find at fairs or parks: a set painted on a wooden board, put your head in the hole, and you've got the body of a pirate, model or folk dancer. In the advertising campaign for the site in question, transavia.com, the decor is vacations: you put your head in the hole, and pretend you're at the beach, on the sea, or in a foreign country. And the slogan falls like misery on the world: "Go away for real." So don't pretend you've left with fake photos - implied: because it's too expensive, but not on our site. But why *leave*? Here again, we get the impression that any normally constituted human being would need to leave: it's Lucette's happiness and it's what makes us unhappy. As usual, happiness is a matter of money. And as usual, under the pretext of selling us happiness, we're made unhappy: by displaying these images of travel, vacations and elsewhere in the corridors of the metro or on 4 by 3 posters along the sidewalks, they're trying to show all passers-by that their living environment is sad, their existence laborious, monotonous, tedious and miserable - in short, that real life lies elsewhere. It's these ads, campaigns and posters that make us unhappy, by making us believe and feel that we absolutely must not be satisfied with life as it is. François Brune says it best: "the worst trouble with the metro is that you can't escape Club Méditerranée[28]".

Above all, this desire for elsewhere and for travel expresses, as you'd expect, a dissatisfaction with the here and now. Let's imagine that on a bus, a passenger spends his time changing seats for no apparent reason - it can happen. What would you think? He's got a problem! At least, he can't find his place, can't sit still: he can't feel comfortable sitting still. In the same vein, Seneca refers to patients "who toss and turn, like insomniacs, trying out one position after another[29]". In short, if you can't stand still, if you always feel the desire or need to change, then you're sick or unhappy. So why should this perpetual desire to *leave*, to go and see somewhere else, appear to us as an image of happiness? If Lucette and her husband spend their Lotto money on travel, it's because they don't like their life here. As we've seen, they're retired, their home smells of mothballs and they're inbreds. Why leave for Australia, only to come back and play again? Rich or poor, Lucette has no life, and is content to kill time, distract or entertain herself. But, as Seneca again says, "once the

28. BRUNE (François), *Le bonheur conforme, op. cit.* page 9.
29. SENECA, *On the Tranquillity of the Soul*, II, 6, *op. cit.*, page 135

2. "That's the game, my poor Lucette!"

distractions have vanished", once back from a trip, "you can no longer stand your house, your solitude, your four walls, and, left to yourself, you look at yourself reluctantly"[30]. In fact, that's why we want to leave right away. But would anyone with a life here want to go anywhere else?

If Lucette doesn't want to go back to Australia, it's because she's already been there, and seen that there was nothing there, or rather, that there was always her. It's your own life, and therefore yourself, that you're trying to escape from when you dream of elsewhere. Thus," says Seneca, "everyone is always running away from himself. But what's the point if you can't escape yourself? We follow ourselves, and never does this heavy company let go of our heels[31]!" Lucette represents the image of unhappiness or unattainable happiness. She should make us realize that the road to happiness is not the same. On the contrary, Lucette and her husband have clearly understood that the happiness of advertising is an illusion, and as Seneca would say, "the adulterated luxury of their existence inspires them only with this cry: 'More of the same! When will it end?"

30. *Ibid,* II, 9, page 137.
31. *Ibid,* II, 14, page 140.

3. "LET'S NOT MISS THE SIMPLE THINGS."

(Does nature have a way of doing things?)

"Isn't living precisely the desire
to be something other than this nature?"
NIETZSCHE.

A little flute tune, a child playing with bits of wood on the banks of a river, and the little phrase, like an ode to the quiet happiness of country life: "Let's not miss out on the simple things: Herta ham". Ah! The real thing! On the other hand, I don't know why the kid is dressed as he was in 1912. It must have been a Parisian agency that did the advertising. Good pre-war flavors, as in Bonne Maman jam: to find them, you don't need a time machine, just cross the boulevard périphérique. Beyond that, it's the *provinces,* which means the countryside, which means the big rednecks still living in the 19th century, without water, electricity, cars or iPhones. There, in the Val d'Oise, Burgundy or Normandy, supermarkets don't exist: people go to the market to buy Saint-Môret, "the cheese-maker's primeur". Girls wear the same dresses as Sophie Marceau or Emmanuelle Béart when they star in a film about the Second World War. The men wear berets or caps, and all look like village idiots. The children play with sticks and are dressed as in Victor Hugo's *Les Misérables. This was* already the case in the advert that traumatized me when I was a kid: "Chavroux, sweet goat's cheese, fresh taste." I remember the father vigorously rubbing his kid's hair. Like the Petit Basque ad, too, with yet another kid wearing a beret and... a sheepskin vest! In the Lepetit ad, "le grand nom du camembert", the designers really take us back to the 19th century, to 1872, when great-grandfather "Auguste Lepetit" was refining his first cheeses. He makes his son smell a Camembert - again: "tu vois fiston, etc." (you see, son, etc.). It's a bit sad to know that outside Paris, children are still working, while back home, they're happy: they eat Nutella and go to school. To tell the truth, you can't really see the difference between the 19th century and today in their ads. In the provinces, in the countryside, *we don't live like gentlemen*, we work hard to make good products for us city folk.

Except in the Midi. The provincials of the South are all lazy: they don't like it when you open a bottle of Salvetat during their siesta. They're lucky in the Midi: life hasn't changed a bit since Marcel Pagnol. They make *soap the old-fashioned* way, calling it "Le Petit Marseillais". Over there, they all have such cute singing accents, they put olive oil everywhere, the women hang their washing out in the field, and *everything* smells of lavender. Let's not miss the simple things, the simple people, the provincials, those inbred degenerates. Strange, in the ad's praise for *authenticity* and nature, there's all the contempt, misunderstanding and prejudice of city dwellers for this countryside, where we're willing to go for a weekend, but after Sunday evening, it's boring. A certain idea of what's authentic, what's *real,* which naturally has nothing to do with authenticity - all the more so as it often involves industrial products.

"You see, it doesn't cost any more to eat well."

"Let's not miss the simple things" (and Saint-Albray, "the best things in life are the simplest"). That's what philosophers, whether Cynics, Stoics or Epicureans, recommended to find peace and happiness. "For simple flavors bring pleasure equal to a diet of abundance" wrote Epicurus[32]. You'd think that *haute* cuisine would be better than a Herta ham and butter. But that depends on who you are: it's all a question of habit or *diet.* If you're used to a frugal meal[33] - "it's a dairy product, a glass of orange juice and two slices of Nutella" - then you're in for a real treat. But if you're used to luxury and fine wines, you won't even be able to enjoy them: having fallen into the routine of luxury, *an abundant table* will seem normal and even the bare minimum. In short, if we miss out on simple things, we also miss out on riches, because we no longer feel that luxury is luxury. As Aymé Jacquet would say after kidnapping children and dragging them by force to the Casino cafeteria: "You see, it doesn't cost any more to eat well." This is because pleasure

32. EPICURUS, *Letter to Meneca, op. cit.*, page 49.
33. Contrary to popular belief, a "frugal" meal is not at all "an abundant table", but on the contrary, a light meal.

3. "Let's not miss the simple things."

is always commensurate with the lack we feel, and if we desire little, we can be satisfied with almost nothing: when we're really thirsty because we've been running or it's *too hot to work*, a simple glass of water is enough to produce enormous pleasure. When you're really hungry, you'll eat anything, even Herta ham. And when you've held back from peeing for too long, the release that comes borders on the mystical.

This is how Diogenes the Cynic, who lived in a barrel, chose to lead the life of a dog. Animals are happier than we are, because their needs are natural and easy to satisfy: eating, drinking, sleeping. What's the point of trying to accumulate material objects, like all those cars, smartphones or perfumes? When we always want to have the latest technological jewel instead of settling for the simple things, we're never satisfied: I've got the iPhone 3G, then I'll need the 3G+, then the 4G, then the 5, and so on. Above all, if I can't do without my phone, I'll be very unhappy the day it's broken or stolen. So you feel strangely cut off from the world, and very deprived, the day your phone stops working. And yet, the world is still here, and so am I. All these consumer objects do nothing for us, and to be happy, it's better to get rid of our artificial needs and settle for simple things. It's even said that, "one day seeing a little boy drinking out of his hands", Diogenes "threw his goblet out of his saddlebag, exclaiming, 'A kid has surpassed me in frugality!'"[34]

34. *The Greek Cynics. Fragments et témoignages*, chapter 2, "Diogenes", translated from the Greek by L. Paquet, Le livre de poche, "Classiques de la philosophie", 1992, page 79.

"Mangeons Bien, mangeons Bio, mangeons Bjorg!"

At home, we buy "organic". Why? Because it's better. Because it's better: we have to buy organic - a *categorical imperative.* In fact, we could be sold anything with "Bio" written on it. It's a sure thing in terms of image, and probably the best brand ever created. Can the others claim to have become absolute values that cannot be challenged? We can always hesitate, between Pepsi and Coca-Cola, BM and Mercedes, Chanel and Hermès, Burger King and Mac Do. On the other hand, we don't ask ourselves whether we should buy organic or not. If we don't, it's because it's expensive, or because we're used to it, or because we're lazy, in the same way that it's always a bit difficult to sort our garbage or stop smoking. But we should buy "organic". And yet, we don't know why. It's not so much that the organic label is misleading - is it really organic? Isn't the food industry lying? Yes, they are. But it's rather that we don't even know what the word means. The poet Paul Valery said of freedom: "one of those detestable words that have more value than meaning". And the remark would apply quite well to "Bio".

For a long time, I thought I knew what *bas-relief* meant. I knew the word well because I'd always heard it, and to me it meant a kind of frieze, with figures or scenes carved into the *bottom of* a wall - hence the name. Then I went to Egypt and the guide showed and described bas-reliefs. Not at all what I thought: in fact, *bas-relief is* when the sculpted form (a man, a horse, etc.) is barely distinguishable from the background, when its relief is barely marked. High relief, on the other hand, is very prominent. I'm sure you knew

3. "Let's not miss the simple things."

that. I didn't. And that's when I realized that I didn't know what I thought I'd always known. If I didn't really know what a bas-relief was, it was because I'd never asked myself. And if I'd never asked myself, it was because the word was familiar to me: I knew it well because I'd often heard it, or rather I thought I did, and as a result, I'd never looked up its meaning. It's sometimes said that it's not enough to repeat a lie for it to become the truth, but I think that's wrong. As Heidegger writes in *Being and Time*: "It is enough to speak and repeat without rhyme or reason for revelation to turn into dissimulation[35]." If I come up with a word you've never heard before, one of Heidegger's famous neologisms, you'll no doubt be astonished, and you'll ask me to explain it to you: *Dasein, ontological* or *mundane*, what does it mean? Since we can see at once that we don't understand anything, we're looking for the meaning of these obscure words to be *revealed to* us. On the other hand, words like *subprime, PVC window* or *eurobond are often heard* on TV or in other places, in chatter and conversation. As a result, we don't try to find out what they mean. When I visit an apartment, I ask if it has PVC windows, but I don't even know what *PVC* means, and I don't try to find out. Advertising, the advertising discourse and all its slogans work in exactly the same way: we simply repeat the same little phrases, the same assertions, to the accompaniment of little tunes that get the messages into our

35. HEIDEGGER, *Being and Time*, §35, translated from the German by R. Boehm and A. de Waelhens, Gallimard, "Bibliothèque de la philosophie", 1964, page 208.

heads: "let's not miss out on the simple things", "205, a hell of a number", "bread, wine, Boursin", etc. In the end, we believe what we're told, *for no reason at all,* simply because we've become accustomed to the message and incorporated it.

"Mangeons Bien, mangeons Bio" (Let's eat well, let's eat organic) is what Bjorg tells us, and by dint of hearing that organic is good, we end up believing it, without question. I don't even know when I first heard the word *organic,* or how I know it's good. And yet, I throw myself at the organic aisle like misery on the world every time I go shopping. So, why do you place so much value on "organic"?

"With sugar, you're right on the money."

Organic is good because it's natural[36]. And natural is always better. Here again, it's impossible to list all the slogans that evoke the *natural* origin of their products, whether food or cosmetics. Heudebert, *naturally*. No need to argue. In fact, if advertisers go to such lengths to include a reference to *naturalness* on their products, it's because consumers have a very positive idea of nature. Volvic, "a volcano goes out, a

36. In Greek, "nature", in the sense of anything not made by man, is called "*physis*", a term found in "physics", which is the science *of* nature, i.e. of the laws of nature: gravitation, falling bodies, etc. In French, "bio" refers to life, as in "biologie", which characterizes both plants and animals. In Greek, however, it's the word "*zôè*" that designates biological phenomena. In French, the term is used for everything "zoological", which refers to animals. As for the Greek "*bios*", it doesn't actually refer to biological life, but to a type of life, such as "an artist's life" or "living the good life". "*Bios*" is therefore a life that is neither animal nor natural, but corresponds to a truly human life.

3. "Let's not miss the simple things."

being awakens". And that's what nature is all about: everything that's not made by man, but by the age-old forces of "water, air and life", as the beautiful Perrier advert declaims, with the girl screaming louder than the lion - an excellent ad, really. It was a way of reorienting the brand's communication towards the *natural* side of its sparkling water, after the Benzene-contaminated bottles affair, which was disastrous for the brand's image in 1990 - "Perrier, it's fioul[37]!" It's easy to see why people want to buy organic. Pollution, battery farming, vivisection and pesticides: by dint of investigations, revelations and scandals about the manufacture of food and consumer products, we've come to distrust anything that isn't *organically produced,* where chickens are raised in the open air. "With sugar, you're right on the money." Still, it's better than all those sweeteners, aspartam and other chemical sweeteners with evocative names like E 950 or E 955. In the end, everything man makes is suspected of being bad for health or the environment.

"With sugar, you're in the right", because the natural is always *truer* than the artificial. And yet, the term *"artificial"* refers first and foremost to that which is man-made, that which is the product of art and human know-how. But *artificial* has long been synonymous with *fake*: an artificial flower is a fake flower, just as PIP silicone gel breasts are *fake* breasts - and dangerous to health. As nature is truer

37. A little phrase that was around at the time to pastiche the brand's slogan, which was "Perrier, c'est fou!"

than artifice, it is also more beautiful. This is an old idea of Plato's, recalled by Hegel in his lectures on art: "According to common opinion, beauty created by art would even be far below natural beauty"[38]. It's true that *fake* breasts can be more beautifully shaped than the original - and that's why people want implants. But what's artificial will always be less beautiful, because it's been *remade*, and the woman whose face has been remade isn't *really* beautiful. Only nature *can do* things, whereas human know-how is content to *remake* them, and that's inevitably not as good.

An *artificial person*, too, is more or less *false*, more or less *hypocritical*, and to be someone *authentic*, you have to be *natural*. The famous Le Petit Marseillais soap, in a TV ad showing yet another girl in a little dress in a field of fruit trees, recommends: "Stay natural". Nature is not only the environment we should respect, it's also the model we should follow in our behavior: we need to be natural. Heudebert, "naturellement". In this slogan, we find the ambiguity of the adverb *naturellement*, which means not only *naturally*, but also *obviously* or *it's normal*. Nature is our moral guide, telling us what is the *normal*, right and good way to behave. In fact, when *mainstream opinion* condemns certain behaviours, such as homosexuality, it's because they are *unnatural* - in other words, a *perverted version*. And we hear the famous arguments that a man is *made* to go with a woman, because

38. Hegel, *Introduction à l'Esthétique*, translated from the German by S. Jankélévitch, Magnard, "Apprendre à philosopher en lisant", 2000, page 9.

3. "Let's not miss the simple things."

nature *has made it so that* only a man and a woman can have children. And as everyone knows, nature *does* things well.

"Outwit Mother Nature" (Tampax)

But if Nature's got it right, why try to *outsmart Mother Nature* with Tampax Pearl and its "revolutionary protection system"? It's not me saying it, it's the TV ad: while a girl is having the time of her life at the club, a matron in an apple-green Chanel outfit bursts in right in the middle of the dance floor. "Mother Nature? exclaims the frightened girl. Not now!" The lady holds in her hands a vermilion-red gift-wrapped package. She looks like the Evil Queen who's come to bring a poisoned apple to our modern-day Snow White: "I've brought you your monthly present, darling: your period!" A few grams of finesse in a world of bullies... But the girl has managed to *outwit Mother Nature*: "I can dance all I want, because I've got the new Tampax, etc."

"If the natural course of things were perfectly good and satisfactory," writes John Stuart Mill, "every action would be a useless interference which, unable to improve things, could only make them worse[39]." And if nature had its way, it would be quite abnormal to protect yourself when you've got your ragnagnas. Moreover, in commercials, menstruation never looks *natural,* but is always represented by a trans-

39. Mill (John Stuart), *Nature,* translated from the English by E. Reus, La découverte/Poche, 2003, page 61. An essay on all these issues that should be read in full.

parent blue liquid. And yet, hasn't it been said that nature is the most beautiful thing in the world? Well then! In fact, it all comes down to this personification of Nature in the guise of a *Lady who has* the same characteristics as human beings, who thinks before she acts, and who wants to do things *right*, especially "for us men". But does nature do the right thing? When "a volcano goes out, a being awakens", *that*'s beautiful. But when it ignites, thousands of human beings fall asleep. It's called a natural disaster. John Stuart Mill insists on "the amoral character of nature[40]". Neither good nor bad, nature doesn't think about what it does, and when we talk about nature's *benefits*, we forget all about its harms. In fact, apart from tampons, cosmetics advertisements offer every means of "outwitting Mother Nature", even as they extol the *natural* character of their products, with *essential oils* and other plant origins. Yet the aim is always to fight wrinkles, plumpness - in short, time, old age and death - even though this is our nature. "In fact," Mill writes, "what is obvious is that nature performs every day almost all the acts for which men are imprisoned or hanged when they commit them against their fellow creatures. According to human law, the greatest crime is to kill. Yet Nature kills every living thing once, often after prolonged torture[41]" - because we all die one day, sometimes as the *result of a long illness*.

40. *Ibid*, page 67.
41. *Ibid*, page 68.

So nature doesn't do things particularly well, and the *natural* or *organic is* probably not *absolutely* good. For once, it's Plato's opponents who are right, like the character Protagoras who appears in one of his dialogues: there are, he says, "many good things that are detrimental to men, like certain foods, drinks, drugs and many other things, others that are useful to them, and others that are indifferent to them, but which are good for horses[42]." Nature is indifferent to us, and everything depends on how we use it: Destop is good for unclogging drains, but you shouldn't drink it. It's either a cleaner or a poison. The first is the "deep" or "revolutionary" ecology[43] which advocates hatred of mankind in defense of an absolutely good nature, whereas nature doesn't particularly mean any good to us - nature *means* nothing. This is reflected in the famous term "*artificial*", which suggests that everything man makes is bad.

Conversely, if industry and man's creations can be so destructive and polluting, it's because we take ourselves to be the center of the world, considering that all that matters to nature is the good of mankind. But there are *many good things that are detrimental to mankind.*

---

42. PLATO, *Protagoras*, 333d-334d, *in* PLATO, *Protagoras, Euthydemus, Gorgias, Menexenus, Menon, Cratylus, op. cit.*, p. 65.
43. Expressions taken up and studied in FERRY (Luc), *Le nouvel ordre écologique*, deuxième partie, chapitre 1, Grasset, 1992.

Soleil vert

Green Sun is the sci-fi movie that traumatized me as a kid when I saw it on TV[44]. I remember Charlton Heston in a cap, strolling through a market where there was no fruit or vegetables for sale, only *green sunshine*, a kind of *artificial* synthetic tablet. In fact, the film takes place in the future, at a time when nature has totally disappeared: not the slightest bit of *greenery*, nor any animals. The industrial nightmare of many science-fiction stories. All that's left to eat are these artificial tablets produced by the company Soleil, and nobody really knows what's in them - are they organic? I remember the final scene in particular: an old man is about to die, and like all dying people, he is allowed to end his days in a sort of hospital room, on whose walls images of natural landscapes are projected. I remember these images: an animal documentary, in which we see a doe snorting at the edge of a wood. For us, it's commonplace, but in this future, it's the kind of scene we can no longer observe. These are probably images shot in the past that are being broadcast to the old man. He's going to die, so he's entitled to his *little* virtual *corner of nature.*

Isn't this *the* world? That famous scene in the hospital room, where people are shown images of a nature that no longer exists, sounds rather like all those ads selling nature

44. Originally a science fiction novel by Harry Harrison, published in 1966 under the title *Make Room! Make Room!* But it was only translated into French following the success of Richard Fleisher's film, released in 1973.

3. "Let's not miss the simple things."

and authenticity. In the film, if the old man finds pleasure and interest in looking at images of nature, it's because it's nowhere else. This is the Society of the Spectacle, "where the sensible world is replaced by a selection of images"[45]. If advertising is so full of images of nature, and if it speaks so poorly of it, using bucolic and peasant clichés unearthed from the past, it's perhaps because nature no longer really exists, replaced by its avatar, the image of nature. The ads that celebrate nature are those that destroy it and pollute the landscape with posters and neon signs from JCDecaux & Co. And the desert is advancing, or rather, retreating. Nature is like McCain French fries: "It's those who talk about it the least who eat it the most."

---

45. Debord (Guy), *La Société du Spectacle,* II, §36, Gallimard, "Folio", 1992, page 36.

4. "PRORETINOL 100% VEGETABLE + YOUTH ENZYMES".

(How can you tell a science is a science?)

"How diverse and inconstant are the illusions that flatter the human soul and the follies in which it allows itself to be led." SPINOZA.

The guy in the white coat with the graphics

My first man in a white coat was the man who sold *Le chat machine*: "This little corner of nature," he said, "is the ideal setting to tell you about the new phosphate-free *Le chat machine*." I remember he looked like Dominique de Villepin. I also remember that the ad made an impression on me, because I was told, at the same time, that a Le chat employee had committed suicide by letting himself be locked in a washing machine. I also remember wondering if it used to be serious when there was phosphate. Apparently it was, since it was deemed necessary to remove it. "This little corner of nature..." I immediately understood that phosphate was not environmentally friendly and that Le chat had done the right thing in removing it. On the other hand, I didn't know what

4. "Proretinol 100% vegetable + youth enzymes".

phosphate was. But there are *hs*, so it must be Greek, so it must be scientific.

For example, a good way to sell various, scattered objects is to use scientific words. For creams, in particular, that make wrinkles disappear and promise youthfulness - "Roc, promises kept". To extol the virtues of these creams, we're given substances with evocative names that bring to mind middle-school chemistry and biology classes: liposomes, trace elements, retinol, proretinol, ceramide, enzymes and bifidus, which is more likely to be found in yoghurt - but after all, why not put a little on blackheads, since creams are made with beet extracts. Indeed, when we're not being told the name of an unknown molecule, we're learning about the unsuspected effects of natural products: things made from beet, eggs or whatever. When will we see a revitalizing cream with duck mousse, known for its exfoliating effects? "And to treat wrinkles in depth, we prefer duck breast or confit", why not? In the end, you wonder if you've missed a few lessons. It's all my fault! I probably shouldn't have skipped biology class in high school on October 13, 1986: that's when she must have talked about proretinol and Q10 coenzymes. Indeed, we're often told that these enzymes and other pro-machines *are known* for their effects this or that. So, we ask ourselves: *known* by whom? "Well, science! Scientists!" Fortunately, there are serious students who have become researchers at L'Oréal. Instead of chatting to your neighbor about whether Kevin Tondelier would like to go out with you, you should have been in class!

The implication is that this knowledge is more or less accepted by a scientific community, although it's not clear which one. One gets the feeling that cosmetics and food research, all brands taken together, are the champions in scientific matters, so much so that one wonders why no L'Oréal or Danone laboratory technician has yet been awarded the Nobel Prize. Isio 4 contains fatty acids essential to our health. Yes, we usually add the adjective *"essential" to* say that this is the true reality of the microscopic world that we can't see if we haven't done research in a laboratory. *Essentials*: the idea that we've discovered the essence of reality, the *active principles* of different things, whether living or inert. Above all, it's the idea that we can't understand it, but that it's really scientific. So it's true.

So what's scientific about advertising? First of all, there's the famous professor in a white coat, of Swiss, Belgian or American nationality (to avoid prosecution), addressing the camera from his aseptic office or laboratory. There's Mr. *Le chat,* but also the researcher at Skip's who exclaimed "Eureka! I've found the brand-new formula" in a musical comedy-style commercial. So why do they wear white coats? Of course, it's the scientific guarantee of the product we're selling: detergent, cream or car. The guarantee, not the proof. Like parents who vouch for the rent of their student son. And in the ads, we're guaranteed that it's scientific because the speaker has a white coat. But it's been a long time since the scientific guarantee in advertising was reduced to a white coat. There's also that famous *scientific* vocabulary or language. There are

4. "Proretinol 100% vegetable + youth enzymes".

also numbers and calculations, formulas that seem more or less mathematical, because they have numbers in them: Q 10, Isio 4, etc. There are also percentages that are supposed to *scientifically* measure things like whiteness for toothpastes or shine for shampoos: “80% more shine”. Then there are computer-generated animations supposed to represent teeth, hair or skin on the scale of a scanning electron microscope, and graphs that vaguely resemble those drawn at school with abscissae and ordinates. All this is enhanced by a *cyber* aesthetic reminiscent of *Tron* or *Matrix*, with a black background evoking the infinitely large universe or the infinitely small void, and green, blue or red lines. That’s science in advertising. But is it science?

Adam and Eve among the dinosaurs

An ad certainly doesn’t claim to replace a physics or chemistry lesson. But even so, many ads base the reliability of their products on scientific *approaches*: hygiene and beauty products are “clinically proven” or “dermatologically tested”, even if the word “dermatologically” doesn’t exist in the dictionary. For cleaning products, the test is even carried out in front of the viewer, and for those wary of overly technical speeches, we’re also treated to testimonials from users, filmed hand-held, who express themselves in a very spontaneous tone - but sometimes, it’s still badly acted. The advertising almost seems to teach consumers to trust only what is scientific, and to consume *responsibly*. And so it is that Dominique Quessada, an advertising executive who has turned philosopher, believes he can assert that advertising "contributes to the *positive reception of* science and its *issues*, and to *its appropriation* by society as a whole[46]." So, is advertising a friend of science?

First of all, why should science need the help of advertising to contribute to its *positive reception*? Isn't it big enough to stand on its own two feet? In fact, many people believe the truths of science as much as those of religion. Although science has made many advances that have found various applications, from aspirin that cures a headache to the famous GPS that receives its information from satellites orbiting the Earth; although our daily lives are saturated with techno-scientific objects, that doesn't stop people watching the great paranormal evenings on *Direct 8* or believing in ghosts[47]. For example, I remember seeing a report on the opening of the Creation Museum in the United States, which aims to show, with fossils to back it up, that Darwin's theory of evolution is, if not false, at least questionable, and that it's perfectly safe to assume that the world was created 6,000 years ago by God. I also remember a visitor who was interviewed by a journalist who asked him if he wasn't surprised to see Adam and Eve

46. QUESSADA (Dominique), *L'esclavemaître*, Première partie, chapitre III, 8, Le seuil, "Verticales", 2002, page 152.
47. Jacques Bouveresse quotes Alan Sokal who notes that in the United States, "50% of the adult population believes in extrasensory perception, 42% in haunted houses, 41% in possession by the devil, 36% in telepathy, 32% in clairvoyance, 28% in astrology... and 45% in the literal accuracy of the Genesis account of creation." (BOUVERESSE (J.), *Peut-on ne pas croire*, "Faut-il défendre la religion?", X, Agone, 2007, page 153).

4. "Proretinol 100% vegetable + youth enzymes".

among the dinosaurs, when scientists - surely mad - consider that 60 million years separate the last dinosaur from the first men: "after all," replied the visitor, "we did kill dragons in the Middle Ages"[48]. In fact, it seems that many people are still convinced that the theory of evolution is no more *plausible* than the dogma of creation. George W. Bush, then President of the United States, advocated teaching these two *theories* together to develop schoolchildren's critical faculties: avoid teaching them just one truth, but several *schools of thought*, and let them choose. What we don't say, once again, is that one of these schools is scientific and the other religious. In other words, one is based on a sacred text that demands belief in the resurrection of Christ or the multiplication of the loaves, and the other on methodical, rigorous thinking based first and foremost on observation. So it's worth explaining to people that religion isn't science. And advertising teaches consumers to believe only what is *proven*.

"What if the effects of science abolished the effects of time?"

So we should trust science because it tells the truth? Because it frees us from prejudice and superstition? In advertising, science's only interest is that it has the power

48. In the same vein, a Muslim site similarly entitled *The Creation Museum* announces: "Discover on this site Harun Yahya's work, which totally *refutes* Darwinism, and the latest news and analyses demonstrating the impact of his work worldwide. Note the aplomb with which the scientific notions of "refutation", "analysis" and "demonstration" are evoked, while it's been a long time since we admitted that we had to distinguish between revealed and natural truths.

to satisfy all our desires. "What if the *effects of science* abolished the effects of time?" Lancôme asks its future female buyers.[49] And then you want to ask: what if it didn't? Would that make science less valuable? It would seem that the goal of science is to fight disease, old age and death, by inventing products, drugs and even surgery, to the point of finding ways of transplanting organs, even artificial ones. But is all this really science?

An Yves Rocher campaign states: "The more science advances, the more it proves nature right. But just what kind of science are we talking about? For example, physics or biology seek to understand the laws of nature or of living beings: why does a body fall when you let go of it, and how fast? Why do wrinkles form on the face as we age? So it's a bit silly to say that science proves nature right, since it's *just* trying to understand it. If a scientist can prove anyone right or wrong, it's his or her colleagues who got it wrong. Einstein can prove Newton wrong. But neither of them has ever given right or wrong to nature, since everyone is just trying to understand it. If not, what? We'll say: - there's a universal law of gravitation in nature, but that's wrong! Scientists don't judge nature. He only asks himself whether what he asserts is true or false, and the only evil that exists in science is error.

49. In the same vein, we find: "Science is the future of your beauty" (Dr Pierre Ricaud), "Science has never made you so beautiful", "From science to beauty" (Galenic), "La science en toute confiance", "La science en toute conscience" (Nivea visage), "Contre le relâchement...ma chance c'est la science" (Roc), "Bio performance. Mastering time through scientific efficiency" (Shiseido).

4. "Proretinol 100% vegetable + youth enzymes".

The mathematician doesn't have to laugh or cry when he discovers that a triangle is a three-sided figure. He doesn't think it's a good thing, because he prefers three-sided figures. "The more mathematics advances, the more it proves triangles right..." Does that mean something?

Of course, this means it's better to eat *organic* or use natural products to make up your creams[50]. But these *issues* and questions are not scientific. They are technical problems: what can be done for man? What can be effective for mankind? But a discovery isn't scientific just because *it works,* as science-based advertising claims. Of course, scientific discoveries can be of use to us, and if medicine is no longer the quackery of enemas and bloodletting denounced by Molière, it's because we know more about the human body. But a researcher is not an engineer.

Science does not ask what is good or bad for mankind. In fact, everyone knows that scientific discoveries can have disastrous applications. Physicists discovered the phenomenon of nuclear fission at the end of the 1930s, and without this discovery, we wouldn't have been able to make an atomic bomb. But was it science that produced this weapon of mass destruction? Physicists simply discovered a natural phenomenon, which was neither good nor bad. Afterwards, we may or may not use these discoveries to make bombs or power plants. So we're very much mistaken when we define

50. Yves Rocher speaks of "science at the heart of plants" or "the science of beauty through plants".

the value of science in terms of its effectiveness. Advertising doesn't reveal what's at *stake* in science at all, but what's at stake in technology. Finally, we don't ask people to trust science because it tells the truth, or because its methods are rigorous, and so on. We teach them to trust it only because it's good for them: science brings them *benefits* and answers their fears - of aging or dying.

"What if the *effects of science* abolished the effects of time?" Of course, that would make science quite sympathetic. But in that case, there's no longer any difference between science and any guru promising eternal life.

Alchemy and chemistry

Advertising science is therefore no different from religion: it's a discourse like any other, which claims to heal, if not console, people of their fears, particularly those associated with old age and death. Basically, advertising science is less akin to chemistry than to alchemy, which has little to do with science. Everyone knows more or less what alchemy was: a practice rather than a science, which sought the *philosopher's stone*, to which two main virtues were attributed: firstly, the power to transform lead into gold, or rather worthless metals into precious ones. Secondly, and most importantly, the power to cure disease, rejuvenate the aged and, ultimately, grant immortality. In short, alchemy sought to produce an elixir of long life. And yet, these promises of immortality are also those that make up the content of science in advertising and fuel the slogans associated with cosmetic products,

4. "Proretinol 100% vegetable + youth enzymes".

many of which are more reminiscent of Harry Potter than Louis Pasteur: elixir 7.9, *so elixir,* elixir of life, bewitching vanilla, fabulous plants, vegetable gold, golden red, great red, secrets of essence[51]. When you hear all this, it's easy to see how advertising can pave the way for the *positive reception of* science. But we can't help recalling what Molière said about medicine when it wasn't really a science, and therefore had little effectiveness: "From time immemorial," he has Argan's brother Béralde say, "there have crept in among men beautiful imaginations, which we come to believe, because they flatter us and it would be to be wished that they were true." (*Le Malade Imaginaire,* Act III, Scene III.) Of course, a message promising eternal youth can only be positively received! But this has nothing to do with the strength or credibility of advertising science: it's simply explained by the strength of the desires of those who listen. The same desires that lead many to accept the dogmas of various religions

51. We also find, on the fly: "Biotherm. Votre secret de jeunesse", "Il y a un soin hydratant si magique chez Carita, qu'il se murmure des histoires d'élixir". Capture essentiel by Christian Dior: "2 essential drops to capture youth". Clarins: "With this foundation, look younger every morning", "the radiant power of youth". Clinique: "Youth reprogrammer". - knowing that the word "reprogrammer" does not exist. Diadermine Aqua Capsules: "This is a sample of pure youth". Estée Lauder: "Lightsource. The power to erase the first signs of aging." L'Occitane's immortelle "is a source of youth for your face". "Ricci complexion, a youthful extract. Orlane B 21: "absolute youth cream". Lancaster, Monaco 365 cellular elixir: "What if 3 drops of serum a day could hold back time?" And yes? That would be great! But we've been asking ourselves that question for a long time! The Egyptians embalmed their dead for much the same reason. Apart from that, advertisers are creative people...

promising an afterlife. Without this desire, no medium would be able to make money by offering the return of a loved one within 48 hours, in exchange for a few thousand euros. But is the purpose of science to fulfill desires? When we go to the doctor, we probably prefer to be told that we're in good health. But it's not this desire that dictates the doctor's diagnosis, it's his knowledge. It's hard to believe that the doctor is preparing his patient for the *positive reception of* science when he tells him: - the tests are clear, you have cancer. But this is science.

But if *advertising science* resembles alchemy, it's above all in its language: that famous swarming of liposomes, proretinol and other phytocaffeine which has no other objective than to smoke out the moron. Indeed, what's behind those magic words that sound or sound scientific? First of all, it's often nothing more than a sound that resonates pleasantly with the consumer. When we speak of *bio* or *phyto-machin*, it's simply because these words bring to mind nature and give a product an eco-friendly note. In this sense, the terms used are often simple tautologies that provide no information whatsoever. When we say, for example, that a product contains *zinc mineral*, we haven't said anything, since zinc is a mineral. But *mineral* sounds good: we think of mineral water and nature. We'll also say that a product contains soy *bioproteins*, for example, since proteins are *organic anyway*, given that they are organic molecules. In fact, some pseudo-scientific terms that *sound* like the names of chemical elements are simply trademarks,

4. "Proretinol 100% vegetable + youth enzymes".

like Pro-Lumine or lacnozinc. Why give the name lacnozinc to an artificial mixture of lactic acid (quite harmful, by the way) and zinc? For the sole purpose of inventing a word with scientific overtones. And here again, cosmetics researchers are reminiscent of seventeenth-century doctors who hid their ignorance behind a veil of words: "the whole excellence of their art," said Molière, "consists in a pompous galimatias, in a specious babble, which gives you words for reasons, and promises for effects[52]. Finally, we could point out that products purporting to contain more recognizable substances or *essential oils*, such as honey, caffeine or orchid, are a vast hoax. In fact, these substances are not chosen at all for their virtues, but for their evocative name: nature, freshness, sweetness or whatever sells[53]. Just as an orchid evokes the idea of a beautiful flower, people need to think they'll have beautiful skin. And that's all there is to it. It's a safe bet that no one, not even L'Oréal, knows whether orchids have any effect on the skin. What we do know, however, is that the word *orchid* has a very positive effect on sales.

Similarly, most alchemical works were written in deliberately obscure, coded or enigmatic language. Why was this? So

52. MOLIÈRE, *Le Malade imaginaire*, "Béralde", Act III, scene III, in MOLIÈRE, *Œuvres complètes, II*, Gallimard, "Bibliothèque de la Pléiade", 1971, page 1153.
53. In fact, these substances are often present in minute quantities in the product in question. When we talk about a cream with orange, orchid or other essential oils, there must be 0.1% of these oils in the product. They're there not because they have any effect on the skin, but because it's a good way of showing the word orange or orchid on the bottle.

as not to confuse the *uninitiated* reader, i.e. those unfamiliar with the secrets of the language used to discover the secrets revealed in alchemical works. After all, you can't tell everyone how to make an elixir of long life! In fact, the question arises as to whether anyone was capable of understanding these texts, starting with the authors themselves. One suspects that this esoteric language, reserved for a circle of scholars, was more a way of hiding the fact that there was nothing to know. Basically, the purpose of an obscure discourse is not to lose the uninitiated reader: it serves to make people believe that there is a science and a circle of initiates. The alchemists, for example, knew no more or no less than the famous doctors described by Molière: "Most of them know very fine humanities, know how to speak beautiful Latin, know how to name all illnesses in Greek, define them and divide them up; but when it comes to curing them, that's what they don't know at all"[54]. And what about advertising science? Doesn't it live up to this image? Of course, it could be said that certain products have *proven* effects or that certain substances are chemical elements that exist for science. That may be so. I don't know, though. Is a user supposed to research organic chemistry before using her jar of cream? But even if liposomes or retinol are names that do exist in some *scientific*, chemical or medical language, they're still words that ordinary people and consumers don't understand.

54. MOLIÈRE, *Le Malade imaginaire, op. cit.*

4. "Proretinol 100% vegetable + youth enzymes".

Le malade imaginaire

How can a 30-second shampoo ad replace scientific studies and research? *The appropriation of science by society as a whole* is a fine idea. At least, this was the belief of the Enlightenment philosophers of the 18th century, who saw the spread of knowledge to as many people as possible as a means of ensuring the political and moral progress of mankind. Diderot's *Encyclopédie,* begun in 1750, was part of this movement: to write, print and distribute a reasoned summary of the sciences, arts and crafts. The benefit? We're freer and less gullible. Literally, "the appropriation of science by society as a whole" means that science becomes the property of the greatest number of people, who can dispose of it as they would their own house or car. So, if I have some knowledge of mechanics, if I know how my car's engine works, I'll be able to tell the difference between right and wrong a little better when the mechanic tells me that the breakdown is due to the spark plugs, the battery, etc. So I'm less likely to believe anything.

This is how Condorcet, another philosopher of the Enlightenment, explains the benefits of the dissemination of knowledge in his *Esquisse d'un tableau des progrès de l'esprit humain*: "Every error is combated from the moment it is born[55]." Thanks to the dissemination of knowledge, made possible in particular by the printing press, false ideas are

55. Condorcet, *Esquisse d'un tableau des progrès de l'esprit humain,* "Huitième époque", Gf-Flammarion, 1988, page 188.

“shaken by the very fact that it has become impossible to prevent their discussion, to hide the fact that they could be rejected and fought”. After that, you can replace the garage owner with any religious leader who imposes his power on followers who are prepared to believe anything. Just as a mechanic can invent a breakdown and make the driver believe that he must fix it, so a religious leader can invent misfortunes and evils that only he can cure. Thus, as Condorcet explains, “they imagined a hell of limited duration, which priests had the power to shorten[56]. This is the same manipulation that Molière denounces in *Le malade imaginaire*. It is above all his doctors, notably the aptly named Monsieur Purgon, who assure Argan that he is ill. As a result, they have no trouble making him pay dearly for ineffective treatments that are supposed to cure an illness he doesn't have. But what if he didn't think he was sick? His doctor's speeches would have no effect on him, and he wouldn't let his doctor treat and manipulate him as he pleased. He wouldn't let him give him bloodletting and enemas, and above all, he wouldn't obey his orders. Why does Argan rely on his doctor? Firstly, because he thinks he's ill, and secondly, because Monsieur Purgon claims to have knowledge that only he knows. So, if the imaginary patient were less ignorant, he wouldn't believe those who tell him he's ill, and would know that their so-called medicine isn't a real science.

56. *Ibid*, “Sixth epoch”, page 170.

4. “Proretinol 100% vegetable + youth enzymes”.

The science of advertising has all the characteristics of a false science. If doctors had the true art of healing," wrote Pascal around the same time as Molière, "they would have nothing to do with square caps; the majesty of these sciences would be venerable enough on its own. But having only imaginary sciences, they have to take these vain instruments that strike the imagination they are dealing with; and by this, indeed, they attract respect[57]." After centuries of progress, during which medicine became a real science, based on solid knowledge of the human body, advertising takes us back to the Middle Ages, when people willingly submitted to those who claimed to have sole knowledge. What is this famous white coat of the advertising scientist, if not a new version of Pascal's *square bonnets*? If anti-wrinkle creams and shampoos lived up to their promises, they wouldn't need fake researchers to sell them. Latin or Greek has been replaced by pseudo-scientific terms, sometimes invented out of thin air, but it's all the same.

This portrayal of science is designed to impress the consumer and make him imagine the powers of a product that do not exist. The lofty, jargon-laden discourse nurtures the idea that science can do anything, and that it is only accessible to a select few to whom the rest can submit. What's the difference between the religious man who invents hell in order to claim he has the power to free his followers from it, and the doctor who invents a disease in order to claim

57. PASCAL, *Pensées*, 82, GF-Flammarion, 1976, page 74.

he has the power to cure it? What's the difference between the mechanic who invents a breakdown to claim he has the power to fix it, and the cream manufacturer who uses the fear of old age and death to claim he has the power to remedy it?

When it comes to advertising science, we're all imaginary patients: we think we're sick of our changing, ageing nature, and we're looking for ways to escape it. But the real scientific approach would be to make people understand that time, old age and death are part of the nature of things, and that there's no point in trying to escape them. We are imaginary patients, and we waste the time we have left by spending fortunes, because we only think of the time we don't have left.

5. "Beef, the taste of being together."

"All that we are given to understand,
This is what the divine *means to a given society."*
Max Weber.

My favorite ad is the one that says, "Who eats beef, eats beef!" Firstly, because I understand it well, since I love steak. I've never quite understood the pleasure people take in eating seafood: you spend hours peeling shrimps or crabs before ending up with very little to eat, and on top of that, your fingers smell of tide - and I'm being polite. At least with meat, there's no question: it's all good. And when I eat steak, it's not my fault. "Who eats beef, eats beef! Above all, here at last is an ad that doesn't brag or talk nonsense, like most other ads in which, by the end, you can't even see the connection between the slogan and the salad they're trying to sell us. Like: "Nescafé. *Open up,* s'ouvrir aux autres." Already, how could drinking freeze-dried coffee *in general make you* want to devote yourself to others or join an NGO to save people? And if not, why would Nescafé freeze-dried coffee *in particular* make you more sociable than another brand? What do they put in their coffee? Then there's Hugo

5. "Beef, the taste of being together."

Boss: "Your fragrance. Your rules of the game." Meaning? What game? And what does smell-good have to do with rules? "Yes, but no: it's because it smells like you, so your scent is different from the others. It's a perfume that reflects you and your personality. If you wear it, it'll show everyone that you're a modern guy, up to date and *free* from social conventions." Free from social conventions, but not from consumerism, apparently... And how could a million-selling sent-bon resemble only me?

In short, most ads make a big deal of it, whereas with beef, it's like with Maxwell, there's no need to overdo it. "He who eats beef, eats beef! And there's no objection to that! You can always show that coffee doesn't make you more lovable, or that perfume doesn't free you from social conventions - starting with the one about wearing perfume when you go out. On the other hand, it's much more difficult to show that someone who eats beef *doesn't* eat beef.

So it was not without a certain benevolence that I discovered this other campaign promoting the beef industry: "Le bœuf, le goût d'être ensemble." The famous ad in which angels from heaven push open the gates of hell, no doubt attracted by the aroma of good barbecued beef, headed by a playboy with a well-trimmed beard, who must surely be Jesus Christ - Our Savior! Never mind the radical change in the message: before, it was nobody's fault who ate the beef, and now it's "the taste of being together". But what really catches the eye is the use, or rather, the hijacking of a number of religious clichés: demons in hell, angels in heaven and the temptation of sin.

Except that it's not souls, but beef that's roasting in hell. And it's so good. The image is therefore intended to be more or less subversive[58]. As in many other advertisements, the aim is to overturn the values of good old Judeo-Christian morality. The sins of religion are the virtues of the modern world: gluttony, of course, but also lust, as shown by this joyful company of angels and demons kissing. At the end, it's an orgy, set to sixties *soul* music and sweaty lyrics: *desire me, desire me, as I desire you, desire me and want me.* We've finally figured out that heaven is hell. In short, advertising is the end of religion.

"Des pââteuh! Pasties! Yes, but Panzani!"

"- You see Lord, I live very simply: I make do with a glass of wine from my little vineyard - that's not sinning, Lord... and some pasta.

- Pasta, Don Patillo, yes, but Panzani.

- ... yes.

- Pastries! Pastries! Yes, but *Panzani*!"

58. Why would beef be cooked in Hell, while Heaven would be out of stock? First, there's the grill/barbecue metaphor, of course. But it's undoubtedly because, in a sanitized world that asks us to eat "five fruits and vegetables a day", beef represents all the evils: too much fat, too much cholesterol, and a lot of doubts about the more or less hygienic nature of animal slaughtering - not forgetting the unfortunate episode of mad cow disease. In short, at a time when everything must be "organic", hormone-free, fat-free, and ultimately, nothing at all, beef is Evil! The advertising agency had to start from there. And these angels undoubtedly represent consumers who are coming to realize that, while healthy food is good for a long life, it's tasteless - and up there, it's boring as hell.

5. "Beef, the taste of being together."

At first glance, nothing could be further from religion than consumer society in general, and advertising in particular. Firstly, because the very image of the religious is often hijacked, degraded, not to say blasphemed. In the character of Don Patillo - a parody of Fernandel's *Don Camillo in the Panzani* version, of course - the irony is palpable, and the pasta-eating priest must make the priest-eaters laugh. Advertising seems contrary to religion, at least in its anticlerical aspect. We like to make fun of religious people, priests, monks and nuns, and it's even a good way to make a marketing *splash.* After all, the purpose of a campaign is to promote a brand. So there's nothing like a good polemic with fundamentalist Catholics complaining about an ad to boost sales.

The classic example is Benetton and its "*unhate*" poster campaign in November 2011, with Pope Benedict XVI kissing Imam Ahmed el-Tayeb on the mouth! (How modern of them!) - ah! but I'm a madman! In short, we're shooting the ambulance[59].

In any case, if mocking religion is a way of asserting a brand's *modernity, it*'s because religious institutions evoke the past, like the character of Don Patillo, who harks back to old black-and-white films in which the parish priest was still at the center of social life[60]. Indeed, the *Don Camillo* series

59. They had already done this campaign in 1991, with a priest kissing a nun.
60. The same goes for the nun character, taken from an extract from the film *Le gendarme et les gendarmettes,* who appears in a *Citroën* advertisement: she drives a 2CV cut in half in a film that clearly dates from the 60s, to sell a "scrap-page bonus" promotion. - which also applies to nuns.

revolves around the rivalry between the parish priest and the mayor, at a time when these two traditional authorities held equal sway over the villagers, who were also parishioners. But that's all over now: parish priests no longer compete with mayors, because society has become more *secular*[61]. The church no longer has political power, and we no longer have to pay tithes or submit to a king who derives his power from divine right. At best, religion falls within the private sphere, no longer affecting more than a fraction of the population, and despite the claims of fundamentalists of all denominations, the offence of blasphemy no longer makes sense for a state that supports no religion[62].

"A Coffee Named Desire."

Freud said: "No, the sexual instinct does not penetrate children at puberty (as, in the Gospel, the devil penetrates swine). From the earliest age, the child displays the manifestations of this instinct[63]. For me, the first time this instinct manifested itself was in front of the famous Nestlé dessert advert that was often shown on TV when I was a kid. A chocolate coulis gradually covered a pear, against a backdrop of jerky, heady,

61. This is particularly true in France, of course, since the 1905 law.
62. Of course, it all depends on the country, the culture and the history. Some countries are secular and religious, while others are non-secular and secularized. Some even have the death penalty for blasphemy. But let's just say that this departure from religion or anti-clericalism largely exists in "Western" countries, where advertising is designed.
63. FREUD, *Five Lessons on Psychoanalysis*, Lesson Four, translated from the German by Y. Le Lay, Petite Bibliothèque Fayot, 2001, page 60.

5. "Beef, the taste of being together."

voodoo-dance-like music. And alternately, the silhouettes of a man and a woman licking a spoon, before finally melting into each other. Forbidden fruit, sex and chocolate. As far as I can remember, it was the first ad of its kind. And since then, advertising has had a field day inciting people to *sin*, starting with lust. The advertising metaphor par excellence is sex. Whatever is being sold, be it cheese or coffee, sexual pleasure is promised. As in the TV ad for Sveltesse, *firm and melting*, in which a woman manages to deceive her husband with a yoghurt. She eats her Sveltesse, languorously licking the spoon, and finishes it - or finishes *herself* - just as her husband comes home from work. You can see that her hair is all wet, as if she's just had an orgasm, and the voice-over concludes: - say yes to your desires. After that, there's always the eternal *Carte noire* coffee, a *coffee named desire* that makes brunette models want to jump on you when they drink it - *"try to remember"*. In short, it's all aphrodisiac. The promise is always that the thing will be the best way to get laid: "Audi 100: he's got the car, he'll get the woman"[64].

64. Café du commerce philosophy and two-bit psychology have long presented the car as the substitute, extension or symbol of the male sex. In any case, we all remember that mind-boggling Audi ad: "He's got the car, he'll get the woman". At the time, they more or less said it was sophomoric. But today, nothing has changed: "Mégane. Be reasonable, treat yourself!" And the ad for *Giulietta*, the model hyper-personalized by the Alfa Romeo campaign. Romeo and Juliet - again, a play on words: "Look at me, touch me, caress me, take me, challenge me, electrify me, control me, protect me, love me, relax me. The same goes for Uma Thurman, whose image is not neutral: *Dangerous Liaisons*, *Kill Bill* and even the character of Poison Ivy in *Batman & Robin*, featured in the Schweppes ad. "*Do you like to have Schweppes, just you and me*? Here, the message is no more subliminal than in the Audi ad; less so, in fact, as we begin to explain the metaphor: "*You mean sex, right*?"

For Freud, all desire is basically sexual, and if you want to make people want you, you always have to appeal to the *libido*. In 1909, Freud himself said: “The sun and the wind are hardly conducive to sexual activity in our society[65]. But today, the sun has been replaced by advertising. Who listens to the pope or the priest to find out what they should do? Not many. With the church, morality, or rather the dogmas of religion, seem to have disappeared. Society has, as they say, become *secularized*, and advertising often likes to turn religious values on their head in quite explicit ways.

There are countless slogans that refer to temptation, original sin and other prohibitions of Christian morality to show that vice is a virtue. Of course, this is especially the case in perfume ads selling scent-good whose primary function is to secrete pheromones to attract sexual partners. “Chanel N°19: try to resist it” or “Amor Amor *temptation*: succumb to Cacharel’s new fragrance”. *And the winner is*: “Eden (by Cacharel), the forbidden perfume”. - This is a reference to the Garden of Eden, with Adam and Eve, the forbidden fruit... But this kind of reference can also be found in advertisements for food products, always with more or less clever wordplay. In an advert for Bordeau Chesnel’s délice de Saint-Agaûne sausage, we see a monk kneeling on a prie-Dieu. He removes his hood, and sacrilege! It’s a woman, and what’s more, she’s eating sausage: “Délice de Saint-Agaûne, you’d have to be a saint to resist it.” Advertising thus over-

65. FREUD, *ibid*, page 59.

5. “Beef, the taste of being together.”

turns the *ascetic* ideal of the religious themselves, which consists in refusing the pleasures and needs of the body, like those famous monks who rush to the table all of a sudden because it's time for Chaussée aux moines cheese: "Pardon, but it's too good!" In short, the consumer society frees us from the sense of guilt fostered by the founding myths of religion. More or less provocative images and advertising messages turn our religious culture on its head. Advertising is the original anti-sin, Genesis in reverse, the return to the fold and, therefore, paradise. From now on, everything forbidden is permitted. The watchword is that there's no harm in doing yourself good, and those who would deny themselves are killjoys.

"One Mars and you're off!"

It's hard to imagine a less ass-kissing Kurt Cobain shouting "*Rape me*" before committing suicide. And yet it's his Nirvana band's "*My Girl*" that serves as the background music for a famous advert: "One Mars, and you're off!" A young man knocks on the door of a monastery lost in the desert, after tearing up the photograph of his ex-girlfriend, who has obviously left him. One imagines that since the break-up, his life no longer has any meaning and is no longer worth living. So he comes to this monastery, no doubt to make a retreat and seek answers, or even to join the orders because he's given up fighting. In the meantime, he decides to eat a Mars bar, and when a monk finally opens the door, all he finds is the torn wrapper of the chocolate bar. The young man was gone again. “One Mars, and he’s off again!” The unstoppable comic epilogue: the excited monk picks up the wrapper and throws it into a huge jar overflowing with all the Mars left by previous travelers. This ad is almost a metaphor for all ads: the Mars has replaced the monastery, earthly food has replaced spiritual food. It’s no longer religion that guides men and gives meaning to life: it’s a Mars. So, what’s happened?

When I was a kid, I thought there was a guy in the asphalt under every red light who was paid to push the button and change the light’s color. I also thought it rained when Jesus peed. I don’t remember who told me that - probably someone who wanted to hurt me, or my mother. Since then, I’ve been to school, I’ve had a few experiences, and I know a bit more about how rain can form, and how traffic lights can turn green. In the same way, the beliefs of religion have somewhat disappeared as mankind has grown up thanks to the progress of science. Indeed, believers themselves no longer necessarily believe that the *Bible* tells true stories, and the famous myth of Adam and Eve has been somewhat replaced by theories of the Big Bang or evolution. The ancient Greeks could still believe that a bolt of lightning was caused by the wrath of Zeus, and a storm by that of Poseidon. Today, however, science knows what causes rain and fine weather, and this makes weather forecasts more reliable than those of the oracles who claimed to interpret the *whims of the gods*. As the sociologist Max Weber put it, we finally know “that there is no mysterious and unpredictable power that inter-

5. “Beef, the taste of being together.”

feres in the course of life[66]". From now on, "the secret of the Olympian gods is Ferrero Rocher". The One God raves about a plate of pasta, and the great moral or existential questions of religion such as "What should we do? How should we live[67]?" have been replaced by the question: "Can there be a holiday without Ferrero Rocher?"

We may or may not regret it. Max Weber sees it as the "disenchantment of the world[68]". Because, in the end, a Mars can never replace a retreat in a monastery. Science may well explain how rain and even the Universe are formed, and even how to fertilize human beings *in vitro*. But it provides no answer to the essential question: "Why? Why does the world exist? Is *life worth living*? And isn't it dangerous that human beings have discovered the means to manufacture other human beings? In short, since science has done away with religious beliefs, we can do a lot of things, but we don't know why. No god to guide us. And that's regrettable. For it was religion that answered the big questions about the meaning of life, and neither science nor consumerism can replace it. With a Mars, it's back on, but where? To find out, perhaps we should have spent a couple of minutes in the monastery, just to think a little about the future. What, then, is the place of religion in a society where the gods eat choco-

66. WEBER (Max), *Le savant et le politique*, "Le métier et la vocation de savant", Plon, "10 /18", 1963, page 90.
67. *Ibid*, page 97.
68. *Ibid*, page 90.

lates, the angels eat beef and the priest eats pasta - *pasta, yes, but Panzani!*

Mr. Clean

At the same time, it's hard to get more ass-kissing than the *Benetton* posters. "*Unhate*": a campaign that invites a Pope and an Imam to forget their petty squabbles and kiss each other on the lips - make love, not war. But what's the difference with Jesus' Sermon on the Mount: "Love your neighbor", and above all, "love your enemies"? There's no point in beating up the priests to show that we've supposedly freed ourselves from religion, if we're only going to continue to bend just as gently to the church's dogmas. As Sartre puts it, we find ourselves faced with "a certain type of secular morality that would like to do away with God with the least possible expense[69]". For if God doesn't exist, why should we still obey the Ten Commandments? In the name of what? "Don't do to others what you wouldn't want done to you." And why not? "Because you wouldn't want it done to you. So what?"So, if you do it to others, it's not fair!" But why should it be fair? "Because if you don't, it's not fair. In short, you might as well be talking to a bottle of red Orangina: "But why is he so mean? Because!" In fact, once you're out of religion, there's no reason to follow those great moral principles, those "*I musts*"... And yet, you still want to. Religious faith

69. SARTRE, *L'existentialisme est un humanisme*, Gallimard, "Folio essais", 1996, page 37.

5. "Beef, the taste of being together."

isn't just about believing in God and miracles, or as someone else might say, believing in a "mysterious and unpredictable power that interferes in the course of life". Whether God really did dry up the Red Sea, or whether Jesus managed to turn water into wine, doesn't really matter. It's all metaphors, or *parables* as they say. What counts is the moral of the story: "Thou shalt not kill", or if "someone strikes you on the right cheek, turn to him the other". And from that point of view, we can't really say that we've left religion behind.

I also spent a lot of time watching cartoons when I was a kid. "In a land of all times lives the most beautiful bee", and "this little bee is called Maya". The marvellous world of childhood that preserves a little from the harsh realities of life: bees talk, bad girls are well punished, and everyone is beautiful, everyone is nice. The credits for *Maya the Bee* or *Candy* were sung by high-pitched voices twirling to spring-time melodies reminiscent of the *hallelujahs* I had to endure when my mother dragged me to mass. In fact, if all these songs sound the same, it's because they have the same function: to lull us into illusions. "*Good night little ones*", "*go in the peace of Christ*". It's the same kind of high-pitched lullaby I used to hear in commercials for *Panzani* or *Monsieur Propre*. "Mr. Clean in everything so clean you can see yourself in it."

Mr. Clean: a commercial full of good old-fashioned religious morality. Like all ads for cleaning products, in fact. "Mr. Clean in everything so clean you can see yourself in it". We haven't moved a step forward since Adam and Eve: man is dust, he will return to dust, and it's the woman who does the cleaning. In the wonderful land of advertising, which turns vices into virtues and makes fun of priests, the image of women is as retrograde, or biblical, as ever. She's still the one who cooks, cleans and wipes the kids. And here, it's impossible to give a single example. *All the advertising about housework is aimed at women.* The father of the family, on the other hand, has just come home from work in a suit and tie when it's time to sit down to dinner. Already, this idyllic image of the family conveys the fundamental dogma of religion: you must have children - and if possible, a boy and a girl. God blessed them and said to them: "Be fruitful and multiply". Admittedly, the form is no longer that of a commandment, but the message is all the more effective in that it is habitual: by repeatedly seeing the same image of the family in every advertisement, consumers come to believe that this is the model for normal life[70]. And in this family, as in *Genesis*, the father is at work: "You shall eat your bread by the sweat of your brow." And in this family, the woman is locked into the role God had condemned her to: whore or mother. At best, she's the famous sex object that allows men to sell her deodorant, a car or coffee. In short, she's the damned temptress who drives Adam to eat the forbidden fruit - it's not me, it's her. At worst, she stays at home to do her chores and fulfill her duties as a mother. God tells her: "You will bear

70. Here we find one of the supposed meanings of the etymology of the word religion, "*relegere*": to bind together. With the idea that the best way to get a dogma into people's heads is to repeat the same thing over and over again.

5. "Beef, the taste of being together."

children in pain. And Blédina says to herself, "On the side of the mothers." With friends like that *by your side*, you don't need enemies. Blédina sells baby food. And what's to stop the father from feeding his kid?[71] And why can't a woman be anything other than a mother? It's no longer a punishment, it's a given. In fact, these great founding myths of religion that we think we've got rid of still dictate our thoughts and conduct, without us even knowing it. "Mixa Bébé: gentle on babies, gentle on moms"[72].

"Open up to others."

To commemorate the death and *resurrection* of Jesus, Christians celebrate the Eucharist: they share bread and wine, which are supposed to contain the body and blood of Christ. But since the advent of advertising, bread and wine have become more reminiscent of Boursin[73]. In any case, how can a wafer that tastes like an ice-cream cone be transformed into Jesus with a wave of a magic wand, or a blessing from a priest? This specifically religious tendency to attribute powers to objects that they don't have - to imagine that Jesus teleported himself *into* the bread - is what Marx

71. Meanwhile, males are reassured of their virility. In this car ad: "Fathers will always be men. This precaution is never taken with women, and the slogans are always something like: "Women will always be mothers.
72. We're just stating the obvious. On the question of the basis of this idea that women should be reduced to household chores, see VERVISCH (Gilles), *Comment ai pu croire au Père Noël?*
73. It's the first TV ad in France, I think.

and others call *fetishism*. It's what we find in our superstitious impulses of weakness, when we become attached to a number or a *fetish* object. We tell ourselves, without really believing it, that it possesses certain powers, that it brings us good luck, and indeed, La Française des jeux plays a little on these remnants of naivety when it launches its Friday the 13th super jackpots. So we can make fun of these old beliefs.

But what's the difference between Zeus, who produces lightning when he's angry, and Mr. Clean, who makes everything shine? What's the difference between a sun God who goes to bed when he feels like it, and Mr. Cholesterol, in his ridiculous yellow leotard, who rubs his hands when he sees people eating butter? It's not because science is advancing *in its own corner* that most people no longer believe in magic, and above all, that we don't talk to them as if they were ignorant. You may say that we don't believe in it: we know that cleanliness or cholesterol are not people. It's an image, a metaphor or a *parable,* as they say. What counts is the message. So, as in religious texts. And as in religion, there's a lot of fetishism.

That's what we're seeing in this famous Nescafé, which is all about "*opening* up to others". Initially, Nescafé is a granulated beverage to be drunk with hot water. It can replace coffee when you're thirsty, and at best, it wakes you up - although this remains to be proven. The *use value* of Nescafé, as Marx calls it in *Capital,* is therefore quite limited. What use are the more or less material objects we buy? That's what their *use value* tells us: coffee is for drinking, beef is for eating, and a

5. "Beef, the taste of being together."

car is for getting from point A to point B. A household cleaner removes dirt and grime, and a car is for driving. A household cleaner removes stains, and perfume makes you smell good. Now, how much does all this cost? What should be the price or, to put it like Marx, the *exchange value* of a coffee, a car or a perfume? Nothing to do with their usefulness. In fact, a perfume costs a lot more than a steak, even though it's less useful: we need to eat to live, but not necessarily to smell good. In fact, the *exchange value* or price of things depends more on the work involved in making them. It's easier to harvest coffee beans than to assemble a car. And if perfume is so expensive, perhaps it's because it required a great deal of knowledge and research to develop. Above all, it's because it bears the name of a *great* couturier like Hugo Boss or Coco Chanel. It's all the work, all the imagination, all the fame of the fashion designer that's sold in a bottle of perfume. In the end, the sweat of Hugo Boss *is* in perfume as the blood of Jesus is in wine. The value we place on consumer goods is in no way inferior to the magic of sacred relics: "You have to look for it in the cloudy region of the religious world[74]".

And, of course, advertising adds insult to injury. It completely fetishizes the world of consumer objects, attributing to them a whole host of powers that bear no relation to their usefulness. Through advertising, objects end up representing much more than what they are: drinking Nescafé

74. Marx, *Le Capital*, Livre I, première section, IV, translated from the German by M. Rubel, Gallimard, "Folio Essais", 1968, page 154.

means *opening up to others,* and smearing yourself with Hugo Boss means being free - *your rules of the game.* The list could go on and on. What's certain is that this *discourse on the object,* repeated and hammered home like a religious dogma, which encircles and frames us without our being able to escape it, we end up believing it. We don't buy Hugo Boss perfume to smell good: it's because it's the cool, porno chic fragrance for androgynous models who are flat and pout while speaking English.

Advertising is the opium of the people (obviously)

Who listens to the pope or the priest to know what to do? We can pretend to rebel when he opposes condoms or abortion. But today, his word carries little weight against that of advertising. It's "Carrefour, je positive!" the new gospel, the new catechism, with its share of opprobrium cast on those who don't respect dogma, and make the mistake of paying too much! That's what sin is today, as in this advert for the price comparison site Kayak.fr: "Mr. what's-his-name paid way too much for his plane ticket". And black sheep or lost sheep are singled out.

You don't have to be a prophet or a priest to preach sermons and enslave people. When Steve Jobs died, the *Metro* newspaper headlined: "The world mourns its supreme geek"[75]. This umpteenth two-bit pun on the supreme guide is a good illustration of the *religious* nature of consumer

75. *Métro*, Paris, n° 2078 of Friday October 7, 2011.

5. "Beef, the taste of being together."

society. It's hardly metaphorical to speak of Steve Jobs as a guru or a prophet, and his grand masses to launch his new products, and his great pseudophilosophical phrases, were reminiscent of Jesus' famous Sermon on the Mount. Except that the aim was to launch a new consumer object and, if possible, to ensure that everyone had the same one - iPod, iPhone or iMac. It worked quite well[76]. We saw people paying homage to their prophet and coming up to him to say *thank you*: thank you for selling them Apple products. Thank you for taking their money and making lots of it. Thank you for making people feel obliged to buy smartphones. And thanks for keeping the monopoly. We get the prophets we deserve. If Steve Jobs has managed to pass for a supreme guide or beacon of humanity, it's because religion hasn't disappeared: it's moved on. All the attitudes typical of religion can be found in the consumer society, for which advertising is Scripture, the sacred book. It spreads the word, disseminates dogma and dictates behavior.

What is religion? The etymology of the word itself is somewhat debated. It could come from the Latin *religere,* meaning to *connect,* either people to each other, or people to God. And today, God has been replaced by Nokia: "*connecting people*". But according to Marx, religion is "the opium of the

76. In *Le Monde* on April 9, 2012, we learned that Tim Cook, successor to Steve Jobs was "the highest-paid American boss", having earned 376, million euros for the year 2011. He can light a candle in memory of Steve Jobs, who secured his future.

people": just as drugs enable us to escape from a reality we find hard to bear, so religion is a smokescreen that promises illusory happiness in the afterlife. But that doesn't change the reality. The drug addict doesn't get better, he just *feels* better. It's even worse: the drug addict is dependent on his daily dose, just as the believer is subject to the dogmas of religious power. Similarly, advertising is the opium of the people: it invades space, streets, TV and computers with images of happiness. All brands and advertisers want only the best for us: "Orange customer service, satisfied when you are". With every step we take, we are constantly presented with an enchanted world that makes us forget that we are slaves to this consumer society.

6. "I DECLARE WAR ON BRITTLE HAIR AND DRY ENDS!"

(Has advertising replaced politics?)

"I want to imagine the new features Despotism could happen in the world."
TOCQUEVILLE.

"In the good thatched cottages, there's *the milkmaid*": plain yoghurt, vanilla flavor or crème caramel. A band of peasants armed with pitchforks vociferate and march through narrow streets reminiscent of cloak-and-dagger films starring Jean Marais. They're shouting *"à la bastille"* or something like that. So the scene is set in 1789. But all of a sudden, everyone stops: silence. They lower their weapons and change direction. What was the event that led them to renounce such violence and hatred, changing the course of history in the process? What did they see? Nothing. They smelled a yoghurt prepared with love. They let their sense of smell guide them as to where this lovely bouquet might have come from, and found themselves - oh, how wonderful! - under the window of the milkmaid, hard at work in her kitchen. It's the same as in Vermeer's painting: *the milkmaid*. So, everyone decides to go into the kitchen to taste her yoghurts. "The story will wait until I've finished this crème caramel". In short, just as cheese can lead a monk to renounce his vows - "I'm sorry, but it's too good" - so can yoghurt.

Vermeer was painted a hundred and fifty years before the French Revolution, and he was a Dutch painter. Apparently, history classes will have to wait and see. "Yes, but it's all the same! It's the time of Jean Marais. That's *before*." Of course, the point is to show that the desserts of the La laitière brand are prepared as in the good old days, with a ladle. These yogurts have the authentic taste and flavor of good old-fashioned products that weren't industrially produced and wholesaled in supermarkets - even though la laitière desserts are industrially produced and wholesaled in supermarkets. But from here on in, the ad suggests that the Revolution belongs to the past: if *Mars* has replaced the monastery, yogurt dispenses us from politics, and crème caramel is the end of the story.

That's right! History is all the changes that have taken place in human societies over time. The question is, why do societies change, over and over again: why do human beings have a history? In *The Manifesto of the Communist Party*, Marx believes he can answer: "the history of every society down to the present day is the history of the class struggle[77]." Class or not, it is indeed the struggles or conflicts between men that

77. Marx and Engels, *Manifesto of the Communist Party*, translated from the German by M. Tailleur, Éditions sociales, 1983, page 30.

seem to explain what happens in history. If everyone were happy with the society in which they live, no one would want to change anything. What's more, at school, history lessons are reduced to the history of wars: the Roman conquests, Charles Martel at Poitiers, 1515, Marignan, the French Revolution and the Second World War. We also learn that it was mainly kings, emperors and presidents who would cause these wars, or who could bring peace: Clovis, Charlemagne, Louis XIV, Napoleon and Hitler. In short, historical events are always political events.

But what if there were no more wars? What if all societies were peaceful and happy? We'd be bored stiff[78]. In any case, politics would be pointless, and that would be the end of history. The goal so sought-after through centuries of war and political strife would finally be achieved: happiness for all.

And that's what milkmaids are all about: the end of history. Crème caramel reconciles everyone: it establishes peace and harmony, better than any political regime that has ever attempted to do so, starting with the French Revolution, which, under the pretext of ensuring the happiness of all, ended up instituting the Terror - like all powers that claimed

78. For Pascal, politics and all these wars are nothing more than entertainment: "When I sometimes set myself to consider the various agitations of men and the perils and pains to which they expose themselves, in court, in war, from which spring so many quarrels, passions, bold and often evil undertakings, etc., I discovered that all the misfortune of men comes from one thing, which is not knowing how to rest, in a room, (*Pensées*, 139, *op. cit.*, page 86).

6. "I declare war on brittle hair and dry ends!"

to establish the happiness of all. Apparently, political struggles have never led to anything, and in fact, we no longer *believe* in them. Advertising is much better at satisfying people's needs and desires, and the consumer society makes them happy.

Long before the French Revolution, the famous author of *L'Esprit des lois* had already understood that commercial relations were the best way to put an end to wars: when one wants to sell yoghurts and the other wants to buy them, they have to get along. "The natural effect of trade is to bring about peace"[79]. But politics always leads to conflict: we defend a party, an ideology, we oppose each other, even in the name of *democratic* debate. And even when we agree, we have to pretend we don't, to mark our difference and win elections.

"Defend your purchasing power."

"I declare war on brittle hair and dry ends!" Not everyone has the same problems in life. Back in 1996, Kate Moss devoted herself primarily to fighting damaged hair. Fortunately, she had found a powerful ally: elsève by L'Oréal. It's true that washing your hair is a bit of a limited project.

---

79. MONTESQUIEU, *De l'Esprit des Lois*, tome II, livre XX, "Classiques Garnier, 1961, page 8. A few years later, Benjamin Constant, another great liberal, wrote much the same thing: "War therefore predates commerce. One is the 'savage impulse, the other the civilized calculation. It is clear that the more the commercial tendency dominates, the more the warlike tendency must weaken. The sole aim of modern nations is rest, and with rest, ease, and as the source of ease, industry." *Écrits politiques*, Gallimard, "Folio Essais", 1997, page 130.

Advertising regularly uses political language in ways that can seem downright ridiculous. Starting with calls for revolution: "Smirnoff. The Russian Revolution." The slogan is based on a vague association of ideas: Smirnoff is Russian, and Russia means Soviet revolution, as if the country had brought the world nothing but communism and vodka. More wordplay, with the Lexus hybrid car: "The silent revolution is underway. And the Freebox "revolution" that makes TV, telephone and Internet reception cheaper and faster. So we use big words to present the release of a car or an Internet package as a historic event. However, it's rarely over shampoo that people start a revolution, and political action isn't really about handing out vodka to everyone. As usual, we fail to see the connection. In advertising, the cause is often derisory, and the revolution is ultimately about consumption: "I declare war" means "I buy shampoo". Even when the message takes on the air of political commitment, it's dubious, notably with those famous Benetton campaigns, against racism, against anorexia and for love between peoples, where we see political leaders kissing each other - and not just the Pope. After all, Benetton is only ever a seller of brightly colored textiles, and it's hard to see what a clothing brand could contribute to world peace.

But is politics reserved for the state, governments and elected representatives? What is politics? What is its purpose?What is the end of political association?" Rousseau asks in The *Social Contract*. And he answers. "It is the pres-

6. "I declare war on brittle hair and dry ends!"

ervation and prosperity of its members[80]." Conservation, like *the instinct for self-preservation,* means keeping ourselves alive. And in this sense, political power is at least expected to guarantee people's security and provide them with the means to meet their needs: food, shelter, etc. As for *prosperity,* that's less clear. But let's say it's about enabling people to be happy, and that's what all governments claim to do. It's not enough to live, you have to live well. So what exactly should politics be about? It's hard to say. In fact, this is what divides the various political currents, such as *the left* and the *right*: some believe that the state should not intervene in economic life, and should leave each person to set up *his or her own small business.* For others, it should ensure social justice. As Rousseau put it: "One is happy when money circulates, the other demands that the people have bread. So it's hard to define the proper domain of politics: basically, anything can be *political.* And isn't the *prosperity* we expect from a government also brought to us - and much better - by all that advertising sells us? And aren't advertising slogans as good as political speeches?

"Leclerc. Defend your purchasing power. After all, this is one of the main demands of citizens or voters, and an ambition - or at least, a promise - of political action. So aren't those who sell us consumer products, the very people who set prices, in a better position than a government to influence purchasing

80. ROUSSEAU, *Du contrat social,* Livre III, chapitre IX, GF-Flammarion, 1992, page 112.

power? And the pharmaceutical industry, which develops and distributes medicines, is perhaps better placed than a Ministry of Health run by technocrats who know nothing about it: Biogaran, "Your health is precious to us". For retirement, instead of a major reform on which nobody agrees, there's MMA, the mutual insurance company that's "solid enough in the current context to ensure the future". - Who are the *customers*? We are!" For transport, we can turn to the SNCF, because "progress is only worthwhile if it is shared by all." And when it comes to settling the debate between nuclear power and environmental protection, EDF is undoubtedly the most knowledgeable - that's their job: "Giving the world the energy to be better." These are not just slogans. The brands that advertise in this way are indeed engaged in an activity that seems to fall under the heading of *politics*. In short, the state may not be the only or the best placed guarantor of *the preservation* or *prosperity of* the members of society.

"All united against the high cost of living!"

Aurélie worked at Biogaran. In marketing or something like that. She has two children. And she told me that her second birth went better than her first, because the private clinic treated her much better than the public hospital. This is normal: a clinic has to offer the best service to its customers if it wants to attract others. At a public hospital, the patient pays nothing, and the staff always receive their salary.

Of course, Biogaran laboratories would be more honest if they said: "Our profits are precious to us. As for Leclerc, their

6. "I declare war on brittle hair and dry ends!"

aim is probably less to defend your purchasing power than their sales. But that doesn't change the fact that looking after their own interests is the best way of defending the health and purchasing power of our customers. It's easy to believe that a government only acts for the good of all, and not in its own self-interest, unlike all those advertisers whose sole aim is to make money. But as Adam Smith, the eighteenth-century Scottish philosopher and father of liberalism, put it, the best way to ensure the good of all is for everyone to look only to their own interests. "It is not from the benevolence of the butcher, the beer merchant and the baker that we expect our dinner, but from the care they take of their own interests.[81] Similarly, if the aim of Leclerc or Biogaran is to maintain or increase their sales, they will have an interest in satisfying the desires and needs of their customers, and not disappointing them, so that they continue to buy from them, instead of going elsewhere. As another SNCF slogan so aptly puts it: "It's up to us to make you prefer the train". Otherwise, you'll take the car or the plane, and we'll lose money.

In the end, this little exchange of courtesies seems more effective than any political action. After all, each of us is in the best position to know what's in our own best interest, what we need and what we want. On the contrary, can a government claim to decide what's best for me, in my place? Why should a political power stand between people, telling some what

81. Smith (Adam), *The Wealth of Nations*, Volume I, Book I, Chapter II, GF-Flammarion, 1991, page 82.

they should sell, and others what they can buy - if not to help itself in the process by imposing taxes? The happiness or, as Rousseau would say, the "prosperity" of the members of a society can hardly be a matter for the state. And as Rousseau says, happiness is a personal feeling "which no one can judge but the one who experiences it; no one can therefore decide with certainty that another is happy[82]". Happiness is undoubtedly not the same for everyone, and while some like to take the train, others prefer the car or the plane. So how can a state act in the interests of "public happiness" or the common good? Those who govern make rules and laws for their own benefit. They are bound to impose *their* vision of happiness on everyone. But by what right? The best thing is to let people do what they want. Otherwise, we infringe on their freedom and, in the end, they're unhappy.

That's probably what all those ads proclaiming the revolution are all about. It's all very well to make fun of Kate Moss for "declaring war on brittle hair and dry ends". - yes, yes, we can. But it's also an ironic jab at politics itself, which pretends to serve the general interest with demagogic rhetoric. "I declare war on brittle hair and dry ends", means *always cause.* What advertising is telling us is that we no longer believe in politics, and rightly so. Smirnoff's famous *Russian revolution makes a* mockery of the 1917 revolution, which only led to Stalinism on the pretext of bringing happi-

82. ROUSSEAU, "Du Bonheur Public", *in Œuvres complètes*, III, Gallimard, "Bibliothèque de la Pléiade", 1964, page 510.

6. "I declare war on brittle hair and dry ends!"

ness and freedom to everyone. And in the end, a vodka keeps its promises better - but that's because we don't expect much from it. Even more clearly, Peugeot says of its 405: "Today's revolution isn't red, it's green. The political battle is over, and the efforts of a carmaker are more useful and effective than all the Grenelles de l'environnement. Contrary to what we learn at school, it's not just politics that makes history. At least, it won't be politics any more. With the Lexus *full hybrid,* "the silent revolution is underway. And why not? After all, technical inventions have also marked the progress of history, without the noise and fury of political revolutions. The Stone Age, the Iron Age, writing, printing, the Industrial Revolution: these are just some of the periods and changes that have brought mankind greater knowledge, happiness and freedom.

"Intermarché s'engage": "Tous unis contre la vie chère! Advertising is the best way to fight for the common good. No party, no class that seeks to seize power to defend its own interests by making everyone else believe that it cares about the general interest. Advertising is a society finally freed from political ideologies, which caters for everyone without forcing anyone to pay taxes or pass laws. To paraphrase Rousseau, we could say that thanks to advertising, society "has no confused, contradictory interests, the common good is evident everywhere"[83]. "All united against the high cost of living! Because it's in the seller's interest, as well as

83. ROUSSEAU, *Du contrat social,* Livre IV, chapitre I, *op. cit.*, page 133.

the customer's. The common good is *evident everywhere*: it is displayed, announced and promoted. And if the happiness on offer doesn't suit you, you can always go elsewhere.

"Who are the customers? We are!"

I had four hours to kill in La Rochelle before getting back on the train. As I was carrying a huge backpack, I decided to sit down at a café. The waiter approached with a big smile, and asked me, hyper polite, hyper nice: "What would you like to drink?" I order an overpriced Coca-Cola, which he brings me *straight away*, as friendly as ever - but with that slightly forced manner of all waiters, quite unpleasant. When it's time to pay the bill, he even has a kind word for me as he takes the bill before giving me my change. We have a few laughs and get on well. So I said to myself: "Well, maybe I could take advantage of this new-found complicity to ask him a little favor: Excuse me, would it be possible for you to keep my big bag behind your counter for an hour or two, so that I can take a stroll around town while I wait for my train? Obviously, he said no. All of a sudden, his tone changed: he wasn't so friendly and kind anymore, because I was asking him to do me a favor for free. He told me that a guy had asked him once before, only to come back with the police and accuse the waiter of stealing his bag. In short, nonsense: too selfish, too self-interested to be of service. Too guilty, perhaps, not to make excuses. And that's often the case: in most stores and restaurants, there's often a sign announcing that "the house no *longer* accepts checks". In case you didn't understand, some of them justify

6. "I declare war on brittle hair and dry ends!"

themselves: "due to numerous unpaid bills, fraud, bounced checks, etc., the house..." The truth is, they've never accepted cheques, and they give themselves good reasons, because they know it doesn't help anyone.

In the end, purely commercial relationships are very false and don't last long: there's no longer any point in paying attention to the other when he's no longer of any use. And even Montesquieu understood this. "We see," he writes, "that in countries where the spirit of commerce is the only thing that affects people, all human actions, and all moral virtues, are traded: the smallest things, those that humanity demands, are done or given for money." [84] And that's what the world of advertising is all about: seducing customers, baiting them, fishing them out, in the sole hope of taking money from them, which is truly immoral. "Orange service: satisfied when you are. In fact, we're taken for cash cows, wallets, and nothing in this debauchery of smiles and kindness resembles what a political relationship between equals should be. Not the slightest respect for the human being, who can just as well die as soon as he or she is no longer of any use.

MMA. "Who are the customers? We are!" It's because we're customers, because we pay money to Mutuelles du Mans, that our retirement is so *precious to* them. But we're not just customers: we're people, we're workers, we're even citizens - why not? Literally, a citizen is part of a city, a state, in short, a community. But can relations between members

84. MONTESQUIEU, *De l'Esprit des Lois*, tome II, livre XX, *op. cit*, page 9.

of a society be reduced to commercial exchanges between sellers and customers? Is this the end of the story, the ideal world in which everything can be bought and sold, in which everyone only cares about others if they give them money, and in which no one is prepared to do a service *for nothing*? Yet the very term *“clientelism”* is used to denounce corrupt political power based on relationships of personal interest, where some people *buy* the votes of others and the support of others. In the context of a political action that should be concerned with the general interest, this kind of relationship is therefore considered immoral, and even a crime.

“You can’t imagine what Citroën can do for you. A little, anyway: Citroën can sell me a car, which will enable me to get from point A to point B more quickly. But apart from that? Can Citroën give me the right to vote? Jobs? Quite the opposite: while advertisers are always very attentive to the needs of their customers, they are less quick to serve the interests of their employees - when they keep them[85]. And yet, it’s the same thing: most customer-kings are also workers, and advertising often forgets this. Besides, they have to work to earn the money they’ll spend to buy their car. Isn’t it a bit misleading to say that the U market is “commerce that benefits everyone”? - even if it’s Daniel Prévost - a very nice

85. In her *No Logo*, Naomi Klein points out that brand policy boils down to “zero jobs”: firstly, because production is outsourced to subcontractors in the Third World, and secondly, because large companies such as Nike and Lévi-Strauss are closing their factories in Europe and North America, and laying off workers in droves. See *No Logo*, “Zéro boulot”, *op. cit*, pages 239-328.

6. “I declare war on brittle hair and dry ends!”

guy, by the way - who says so? It benefits the retailer. At the very least, to the customer, even if the aim is to make a profit. But do the supermarket's suppliers, producers and farmers benefit? We're not sure. In any case, Marché U's primary aim is to make money: it's not a *public-interest* NGO dedicated to serving the common good. Far from *defending* the rights that a state can guarantee citizens, Marchés U and Leclerc reduce them to customers, and the only freedom they have left is to buy.

"Take the power", promises Numéricable[86]. It's a typically political, not to say demagogic, slogan. In fact, it's exactly the one used by candidate Jean-Luc Mélenchon during the 2012 presidential campaign. When a politician invites us to take power by voting for him, it's already dubious: the best way to take power is to exercise it yourself, rather than entrusting it to someone else. But when it's a cable TV provider proclaiming "take the power", it's easy to run away. After all, what power does Numéricable give me? The power to change TV channels! The power to press the buttons on the remote control! The citizen is reduced to a customer, and the customer to a spectator. To watch TV, to be a *spectator*, is to observe things from the outside, without participating, without taking part in the action. The "alienation of the spectator", as Guy Debord would say, "is expressed in this way:

86. In the same vein, again for a Citroën car, this unbearable TV ad, in which we are reproached for always saying "yes" to everything, ending with the famous: "And if for once you said no: no to conformism, etc.".

the more he contemplates, the less he lives[87]". And the less he acts. The *democratization of* 3D televisions and cell phones is all very well. But that just means they're cheaper, not that *people* have more power. In short, just because we use the vocabulary of politics doesn't mean we're doing politics.

Even when brands claim to be working for great causes, it's still a way of advertising. There's more to life than posters and TV spots. Brands are also getting in on the act outside the traditional advertising arena, notably by sponsoring those famous short programs that are supposedly of public benefit. For example, France 2's *"émission de solutions"*, which claims to fight for the environment *with Macif.* Worse still, Kinder supports secours populaire by selling *solidarity eggs*, one euro of which is donated to children's aid. The rest goes to Kinder, and above all, this *commercial* operation serves its brand image, which will enable it to sell more Kinder, and so on. Nothing is free. The height of cynicism, but not of Diogenes: generosity, humanity, the defense of the general interest and the common good are sales arguments. It's a bit like Adam Smith's theory reversed: the general interest serves the particular interest. In fact, as someone else would say, "all human actions, and all moral virtues, are trafficked: the smallest things, those that humanity demands, are done or given for money[88]".

87. Debord (Guy), *La Société du Spectacle*, I, §30, *op. cit*, page 31.
88. Montesquieu, *De l'Esprit des Lois*, tome II, livre XX, *op. cit*, page 9.

6. "I declare war on brittle hair and dry ends!"

1984

In 1984, Apple released its Macintosh with a famous advertising film. In a very cold, very blue setting reminiscent of George Lucas's *THX 1138*, troops of soldiers march in step. They take their seats in front of a giant screen on which appears the emaciated face of what appears to be the dictator, the Wizard of Oz, the *Big Brother* of this nightmarish dictatorship. Facing the uniformed and obviously lobotomized assembly, he delivers a chilling speech that evokes the *purification of information*, the *garden of pure ideology* or *the unification of thought*. "Each of you," he says, "is but a small cell in the great body of the State." But someone has entered the main building: the savior, the liberator, the chosen one, who will put an end to this authoritarian regime, like all the heroes of this kind of science fiction, starting with Neo in The *Matrix*. Except that in the ad, the liberator is a woman, which already breaks with the uniformity of this dehumanized male world. Hymn to diversity! She wears a sporty outfit, red shorts and a white t-shirt, which finally brings out the color and contrasts with the ambient greyness. This red is also that of the - Russian - revolution, as the young woman is armed with a large hammer which she manages to throw at a TV screen to make it explode - a symbolic act of the destruction of *Big Brother*. And that's the end. And then a generic advertising message: "On January 24, Apple will release the Macintosh. And you'll see why 1984 won't be like *1984*."

1984 is the famous 1948 futuristic novel in which George Orwell describes a dictatorship led by the notorious *Big*

Brother. In a way, it's *the* model for all futuristic totalitarian regimes: giant posters of the dictator dot every street in the city, and thanks to *telecoms*, the computers of the time, the Thought Police can observe everyone in their homes. *Big Brother is watching*. Fortunately, Apple has announced that 1984, in the real reality of real life, will not resemble the 1984 imagined by George Orwell. On the contrary! The computer will liberate minds and spirits, and the young woman in red is the Mac, another version of La Laitière after all. Gone are the great ideologies of collective happiness, in the name of which a state attacks the freedom of individuals.

That's true. Especially since the Internet has made it possible to disseminate knowledge and information to as many people as possible. Anyone can express themselves, anyone can be heard, and the laws of any country have difficulty applying in these borderless networks. But in the meantime, you have to buy a Mac, and since then, an iPhone, an iPad and so on. "*Think Different*" said Steve Jobs. Think differently, but not too differently: at least think about buying the same Apple-branded screen. In fact, the message worked quite well. This famous uniformity, this greyness, this lobotomy that must force everyone to behave in the same way, we find it quite well with the iPhone. The political horror described by the Apple ad corresponds exactly to reality[89]. As Naomi

89. Not to mention Apple's employment policy. That's not the point, since this is not an economic, sociological or political study, only a philosophical one. See *supra*, note 9.

6. "I declare war on brittle hair and dry ends!"

Klein would say in her *No Logo*: "If this whole revolution is about empowering people, Bill [Gates], why are you closing the market and restricting choice[90]?" And what applies to Microsoft undoubtedly applies to Apple.

"Spam, Spam, Spam, Spam, lovely Spam, wonderful Spam"[91]

When I open my mailbox, I often receive messages from people I don't know, answering questions I've never asked before. "Mr. Vervisch: confirmation of your delivery." What delivery? None, actually. But on the list of all the e-mails the guy is going to send his message to, he's bound to come across a guy who was actually expecting a delivery. And when you read the e-mail, you'll discover a classic advertisement for Vistaprint, a site that makes business cards. One day, I even received an e-mail from a certain Nathalie: "Did you receive my e-mail of September 12?" No. Why would I have received your e-mail of September 12? Obviously, the famous e-mail doesn't exist. But these highly personalized *spam messages,* with the sender's first name, create a sort of familiarity.

90. KLEIN (Naomi), *No logo*, "Zero choice", 7, *op. cit.*, page 206.

91. SPAM is a trademark created and registered by Hormel Foods in 1937, the origin of the name being "Spiced *Ham*" (the product was originally named *Hormel Spiced Ham*). This pre-cooked canned meat was widely used during the Second World War. The association of "spam" and "undesirable" comes from a Monty Python comedy sketch entitled *Spam,* in which the word "spam", referring to the famous canned ham, invades the conversation and menu of a small restaurant (it is included in the composition of every dish and repeated at every turn).

People say, "Did you receive my e-mail? As if we knew each other. But when I read the message from this famous "Nathalie", I could see that she didn't know me at all: "I've been told that you're interested in this and I'm delighted to finally tell you: it's *perfectly* possible today to LOSE WEIGHT fast WITHOUT dieting! Don't give in to fate - you'll regret it - see you soon! This was an advert for the Adelium laboratory. "Losing weight without dieting": that's exactly what the Taillefine 0% girl was selling us. But the form has changed: from now on, the message is addressed directly to me. On the other hand, I don't know who told her I was interested, given that I weigh 62 kilos soaking wet for 1 meter 80. It's kind of the tragedy of my life, in fact: I think I'm too skinny, in short. Adelium's daughter will have been misinformed - but of course, it was a computer sending automatic messages from an e-mail list. Some company must have given them its customer list, which included me, and no doubt *statistically*, the majority of these customers want to lose weight, but not me. That said, sometimes they're luckier.

When I open my Facebook profile too, a whole column of ads appears on the right-hand side of the page. "Star Wars fan? Create your own bank card with your favorite character from the Star Wars saga. Open an account for it now!" Why are you being so informal with me? It's probably because, according to the statistics, Star Wars fans are retarded teenagers. But they got it right. I made the FATAL mistake of indicating on my profile that I was a Star Wars fan. So you'd think I'd be susceptible to this kind of publicity. I probably

6. "I declare war on brittle hair and dry ends!"

think I'm free when I'm surfing the web and minding my own business: reading an article, watching a video, downloading a song. But all the while, *Big Brother is* watching me, even if he has changed his name to Google or Facebook.

We don't need the *Thought Police* to control thought. The *Big Brother* posters invading the city are the advertising hoardings you can't escape. It's impossible to take a step outside, on the road, in the street or in the metro, without being challenged by advertising. And the famous *telecoms* of *1984,* with which the police still observe the individual when he returns home, are computers. It's impossible to open a page, watch a video or even check your e-mail without seeing an ad. And you'll see why 2014 resembles *1984*. As we all know, everyone leaves a lot of information about themselves on the Internet, allowing Google and others to know everything about our lives, without having anything to envy *Big Brother*. And as luck would have it, the ads each user receives on the pages they visit, right up to their inbox, correspond to the traces of themselves they've left behind. So what's the difference with *Big Brother* spying on everyone's life?

Advertising loves to extol all the benefits that science can bring to consumers, particularly when it comes to slimming or rejuvenating creams - "Somatoline: it's *science,* it works!"[92] But scientific progress also benefits advertising, and here,

---

92. See Chapter 4, "Proretinol 100% plant-based + youth enzymes" (How do you know when a science is a science?).

strangely enough, it's much less boastful. Neuromarketing[93], as its name suggests, is based on neuroscience, the study of how the human brain works. They believe they know how to produce a message that will trigger a particular area of the brain and *mechanically* encourage consumers to buy. What more restrictive *Thought* Police could there be? It's no coincidence that the former CEO of TF1, Francis Le Lay, made his famous statement: "What we sell to Coca-Cola is available human brain time"[94]. Who are the brains? We are! From citizen to customer, then from customer to brain, what's left of us?

---

93. Read ROULLET (Bernard), DROULERS (Olivier), *Neuromarketing*, Dunod, "Tendances marketing", 2010.

94. Interview given in the book Les dirigeants face au changement, and quoted in *Le Monde*, July 11-12 2004: "For an advertising message to be perceived, the viewer's brain has to be available. The aim of our programs is to make them available, in other words, to entertain them, relax them and prepare them between two messages. What we sell to Coca-Cola is available human brain time.

7. "PLEASURE IN TOTAL FREEDOM."

(What is freedom?)

"LIBERTÉ: it's one of those detestable words that have more value than meaning; that sing more than they speak; that ask more than they answer; of those words that have made all the trades".

Paul VALÉRY.

"Cats would buy Whiskas." So why don't they? As the CCC (Comité Contre les Chats) has already pointed out, instead of going shopping, cats, "spend their dough at foosball [...] spend their time smoking firecrackers and climbing the ceiling"[95].

Lucky them. That's probably what you say to yourself in the morning, when you have to leave home to face the outside world, at work or at the supermarket, when you see the cat lying on the floor, where the window is shining: here's one who's going to spend his day lounging, on the parquet floor or on a cushion, only moving, on occasion, to go and eat his mash.

95. Of course, this is the text of a fake Les Nuls advert for "Kwiskas", broadcast on Les Nuls, l'émission.

I'm often astonished by the lively reactions of students whenever animals are mentioned. When I tell them that most philosophers believe that animals are not endowed with reason, they always say the same thing: "That's not true! My cat is too intelligent! You can see it in her eye that she recognizes me; and when she's done something stupid, she knows it." No matter how much I argue, with the help of Rousseau, Marx and Russel, an English mathematician turned philosopher, the battle is always lost in advance. It's the same with freedom: students don't believe that animals are any less free than human beings:

- They are guided only by their instincts, whereas men think about what they are doing.

- No, sir, animals are freer than we are: at least, they do what they want.

The advertising doesn't help matters, since the *creatives* often agree with the students: "Rinti, free to live life to the full as a dog." Rinti is a brand of pet food. And everyone knows what *a dog's life is*: a miserable existence, made up of suffering and poverty. So, since when is a dog's life happy and free? Since the slogan of the Rinti TV ad doesn't say so, we can consult the brand's web pages, which are a little clearer: "Rinti Extra treats with beef or lamb give your dog all the energy he needs to live his dog's life to the full, made up of play, sport and walks." The funny thing is that *you* can replace *dog* with *you*, without really shocking anyone: "Rinti Extra beef and lamb treats give your dog all the energy he needs to live a full life of play, sport and walks. If beef or lamb treats don't appeal to you, you can always replace them with chocolate treats like Mars, Twix or M & M's. It's all the same thing: it's all owned by the Mars group, which sells everything from Balisto to Frolic, Canigou and Pedigrée. And in a way, it sells it all in the same way. Games, sports and walks - isn't that what advertising is all about? In fact, Rinti's sales pitch for dogs is pretty much the same as Nutella's for kids. You know, in that insufferable TV ad with the slogan: "It takes energy to be a kid." And if you look at the text in detail, "energy to be a child" sounds a lot like "the energy he needs to live his life to the full as a dog". Because a dog's life is "made up of play, sport and walks", while children have to eat Nutella "for everything they're going to do today: play, learn, have fun". In short, the same life, the same activities, and the same products. It remains to be seen what this freedom is worth, as we are treated like dogs.

"Let's open up the field of possibilities."

Advertising's big business, and what it sells us most along with happiness, is freedom. And it's quite logical. How can we be happy if we can't do what we want? Freedom is undoubtedly a sine qua non of happiness. "For what does a man seek? asks the Stoic Epictetus. To live calmly and happily, to do whatever he wants without being prevented or forced from doing so[96]."

96. *Entretiens*, IV, I, 46, quoted by C. Chrétien, in Epictète, *Manuel*, Introduction, Hatier, "Profil d'une œuvre", 1988, page 14.

7. "Pleasure in total freedom."

In fact, the punishment that men most often inflict on other men to make them unhappy is the deprivation of freedom: from the teenager who is forbidden to go out by his parents and must stay in his room, to the criminal sentenced by justice to a term of *imprisonment*. In short, everyone understands that a free man is happier than a slave or a prisoner. And when a people makes a revolution, what it demands above all is freedom. But what is freedom?

"Freedom is an abstract idea until you find yourself behind the wheel of a Frontera." Fortunately, advertising solves all philosophical problems, which isn't surprising, given that advertisers work on *concepts* - or so they think. With them, you're always free. Even if, as usual, it sometimes takes a big stretch of the imagination to see the connection between what they're selling us and freedom. "Freedom is an abstract idea until you find yourself behind the wheel of a Frontera. After all, why not: the car is what allows the teenager to no longer depend on those famous parents - his *daron* and his *daronne* - who do nothing but send him to his room to deprive him of outings. Thanks to the car, you can drive for miles on end, alone, in the middle of wide-open deserts, just like in all those car commercials, with your music and your phone. It remains to be seen whether this freedom isn't an illusion, given that in real life, we spend hours in traffic jams. But that's another question.[97] Then there are the mobile and

97. See VERVISCH (Gilles), *Tais-toi et double!*, Max Milo, 2011, especially chapter 6.

Internet operators. "Freedom changes with Orange". Here again, paying for a phone or TV package with *no commitment,* and being able to cancel your subscription whenever you want, undoubtedly gives you more freedom. But when Leroy Merlin gets philosophical, the idea is already a little more confusing: "A desire for a garage may come from a need for freedom. It may - or it may not. Let's say it's a garage to store the famous Frontera, at the wheel of which freedom becomes a less abstract idea. It all makes sense.

There will always remain the Hugo Boss mystery: *your rules of the game.* Why is that? In the same vein, Levi's, "One day, freedom will be for everyone." Remember, we're talking about jeans. And what can we say, above all, about the latest TV campaign for LU cookies: "Let's open up the field of possibilities". This time, I'd really like someone to explain it to me: in one of the ads, we see an entire village in the French countryside mobilizing to make a giant screen out of scraps of fabric. In the end, thanks to this great show of solidarity, everyone sits down in the middle of the street to watch a lovely open-air cinema under the stars. But all this was only possible thanks to everyone's contribution: *let's open up the field of possibilities.* It's beautiful. But it's LU. It's for cookies and cookies. You eat them and that's it. So how do you open up the field of possibilities with little butters? "No, but it has to do with the wheat field used to make the cookies: wheat field, field of possibilities. In short, nothing to see. And in the same series, Paille d'or from LU: "to keep the spirit free and light". But what good will eating Paille d'or do our famous prisoner? Even if they have raspber-

7. "Pleasure in total freedom."

ries in them. "Are you sentenced to life imprisonment? Eat a Golden Straw to keep your mind free and light.

But what is this mysterious freedom of advertisers, which can be found as much in a car as in jeans or a bottle of perfume - sorry, a bottle of *fragrance*? In the famous advert for the Zalando.fr website, we discover "an appalling choice of shoes online". It's pretty well done - no, it's not, but the ad is: a terrified boy talks to himself in front of a camera he's holding in his hands, *Blair Witch Project*-*style*. What's he afraid of? His girlfriend's shoes invading his house: "Look at that: shoes, shoes and more shoes! It never stops! They've got thousands of models! The embarrassment of choice, or rather, the choice without the embarrassment, since the girlfriend can always return items that don't suit her, free of charge. Satisfied or your money back.

So she can choose to buy whatever she wants *without obligation,* and she buys it all. But since all these shoe models are screaming with pleasure, she doesn't send any of them back. It's an invasion. In short, the freedom that advertising sells us is choice. So, a simple question: to be free, is it to have a choice?

Buridan's donkey[98]

Taillefine 0%: "Pleasure with complete freedom". Why *freedom*? Firstly, because we have a choice. The TV ad shows us the different flavors: lemon, vanilla, chocolate, and so on.

---

98. Originally, Buridan was a philosopher of the Middle Ages (1300-1358). But most commentators fail to see why this donkey story is associated with his name, given that he himself never mentioned it.

Just great! It's true that being able to choose between several flavors of yogurt is the highest degree of freedom, and an absolute bulwark against all infringements of human rights. Not only to be able to choose, but also to be able to change one's mind. To make choices that don't commit you to anything, by simply following your desires. In the ad, we see a girl - another girl, apparently, fickleness is a feminine flaw - a girl who spends her time changing perfumes: "This morning, I want a lemon Taillefine... quick! A plain Taillefine. But no! Framboise..." A certain way of understanding the Stoic: "do whatever you want without being prevented or forced to do it". To do whatever you want, then, is to give in to your whims, as children are wont to do - and to get them to stop, their parents send them to their rooms and forbid them to go out. And yet, it's this childlike behavior that advertisements encourage when they promise consumers *pleasure in total freedom*. But parents are quite right: if a girl eats yoghurt and really tries all the flavors, she'll be sick in the end: free vomiting. In short, it's not enough to have a choice to be free, or rather, there's no point in having a choice if you refuse to choose.

As we've already noted, "those who want everything want TPS"[99]. The slogan would also work for Canalsat. Incidentally, TPS no longer exists. But it's the same principle: a wide choice of generalist and thematic channels "for the whole family". Cartoons for kids, movie channels for teens, documentaries for mom, and porn channels for dad - but that's never mentioned,

99. See Chapter2, "C'est le jeu ma pauvre Lucette!" (What is happiness?).

7. "Pleasure in total freedom."

especially not in the Canalsat Christmas ads with the singing reindeer. In any case, if there's one thing I've noticed, it's that you can't want it all. At least, you can't have everything. For one thing, the choice isn't so *magical*: some nights, even with three hundred channels, there's really nothing. So I find myself zapping from one to the next without stopping on any of them, and in the end, I haven't watched anything at all. But on nights when I'm really interested in more than one program, I zap too, because I don't know which one to choose. It's not enough to have a choice: you have to know how to choose. It's never fun to have to choose, because you always have to give up something. If you want to watch several channels, what do you do? You'd either have to zap from one to the other, or watch the *mosaic*, trying to keep up with everything at the same time. In any case, when you try to see everything, you don't watch anything. The same goes for the Zalando.fr girl with her shoes: she'll always have just two feet - well, I hope she does - and there comes a time when you have to choose a pair.

The story of *Buridan's donkey has been* around since the Middle Ages. In the seventeenth century, the philosopher Pierre Bayle wrote a version in his *Dictionnaire historique et critique*: "A very hungry donkey would starve between two bushels of oats...; for having no reason to prefer one to the other, it would remain immobile like a piece of iron between two magnets of equal strength[100]."

100. *Dictionnaire Historique et critique de Pierre Bayle*, Tome IV, "Buridan", BookSurge Publishing, 2001.

Initially, this story was intended to show that animals are less free than human beings - contrary to what you might think in the morning, when you have to leave home to face the outside world. But here, we see above all that it's useless to have a choice if you can't choose. Our donkey is *starving*. Fortunately, he's spoilt for choice: we bring him not one, but two buckets of oats. The problem is, he doesn't know which one to start with. He couldn't decide, and hesitated until he was starving. In the end, it would have been better to bring him just one bucket. It's all very well to have a choice, but there comes a time when you have to make up your mind: about a chain, a yoghurt or a pair of shoes. Advertising would have us believe that we could always have a choice, without ever having to choose. But if we don't choose, we're not free: we die, or at least, we do nothing. That's what characterizes the wishful: they always want to have the choice. They want to "open up the field of possibilities", without ever entering into it. They never do anything, because they always want to be able to do everything, and so they do nothing. If I decide to watch *The Godfather, I won't be* able to see *an endless day*. To be free is to do what you want, but you still have to know what you want. That's what the girl in the ad doesn't understand. Of course, Taillefine 0% is first and foremost "pleasure in total freedom", because it's 0%, like Kellog's special K, Saint-Hubert 41, Sveltesse, Silhouette, and so on. The ad promises the girl to indulge herself without gaining weight: to satisfy both her sweet tooth and her desire to slim down, in short, to go on a diet *without depriving herself, without prohibitions*

7. "Pleasure in total freedom."

- even though we're not asking her to do anything. But what does that mean? Precisely, that she doesn't have to choose between gluttony and dieting. You'd better know! We're being sold an *appalling choice* as the ultimate in freedom, and at the same time, we're being shown that *the pleasure of freedom is not having to* choose.

Kant's dove

"Pleasure in total freedom"? But who said freedom was pleasure? It's fun to eat Nesquik when "you've got the hots for it". It also feels good to smoke a cigarette, and sometimes I get so thirsty I almost feel like singing, "my shirt for a beer!" That's the slogan of an old ad from the 1980s. But today, alcohol ads are banned from cinema and TV, as are cigarette ads - so Marlboro has fallen back on sponsoring motor racing teams. Why these bans? Because tobacco and alcohol are dangerous to health. And like all drugs, they are addictive: you can't do what you want when you light up a cigarette, because the desire to smoke is caused by craving. And behind the pleasure, there are deadly substances that you wouldn't take if you really had a choice. To be free is rather to have enough willpower to stop: you do what you want because you don't give in to your cravings. And with Nesquik, it's the same thing: you can't control a *huge craving*, and what you feel is an appetite that you didn't ask for. There's nothing pleasant about giving up smoking - and that's why I've never stopped. And yet, suffering is a sign of liberation, whereas pleasure pushes the smoker further into dependence. So pleasure and freedom don't necessarily go together, and as Rousseau would say: "These two things are so different that even they are mutually exclusive[101]."

When I was a kid, we were dragged off to long, drawn-out family reunions on Sundays. So we had to keep busy. With the cousins, we'd often start playing board games like Good Pay or Monopoly. No one ever forced me, and at first I was happy to find a way to kill time. But I always ended up bored, especially when I was losing. I didn't enjoy it anymore. As a result, I regretted having said yes and embarked on a never-ending game. From then on, I felt obliged to carry on, although I would have liked to have stopped. But why was I obliged? I'd committed myself to the game and now the others were counting on me. Could I leave them in the lurch because I didn't feel like playing anymore?

"When everyone does what he pleases, we often do what others dislike, and this is not called a free state." That's more Rousseau[102]. And not Taillefine. The girl in the ad thinks she's free because she does what she pleases. The sacrosanct freedom of the customer-king, who has the right to indulge his every whim, without concern for others. Of course, Taillefine's daughter can always empty the yoghurt aisle if she feels like it. But if it's the famous smoker who decides to do as he pleases, it's obvious that it will upset those who

101. *Lettres écrites de la Montagne*, Eighth letter, in ROUSSEAU, *Œuvres complètes*, III, *op. cit.*, page 841.
102. *Ibid.*

7. "Pleasure in total freedom."

don't smoke. And what happens to their freedom? We may feel that laws prevent us from doing what we want, and that we'd be freer if we had all the rights. But what if there were no laws? I don't like it when my neighbor rings my doorbell because I'm playing loud music at a party: he's preventing me from doing what I want. At the same time, when I want to go to sleep, I don't like it when the neighbor prevents me from doing so by turning up the music because he's having a party. In short, we don't feel free when we have to obey laws, but we're glad they exist to prevent others from doing anything. In the end, everyone understands that these annoying laws allow everyone to avoid suffering the whims of others. Everyone, that is, except advertisers.

In his *Critique of Pure Reason,* Kant tells the story of a dove in flight. It senses that the resistance of the air requires it to make efforts to flap its wings and stay aloft. A bit like a swimmer who has to flap his hands and feet to move through the water. As a result, she believes she would fly much more easily in a vacuum. As if a swimmer could run a 50-meter butterfly in a pool without water. But if there were no air, our dove couldn't fly: it's thanks to air that it can flap its wings and stay aloft. Similarly, we imagine that we'd be freer if there were no laws. But this is undoubtedly an illusion.

The wolf and the dog

There's another animal story that's been around since the 17th century: a fable by La Fontaine entitled *Le loup et le chien (The Wolf and the Dog).*

"A wolf had only bones and skin,
The dogs were on guard.
This Wolf meets a Dogue as powerful as he is handsome,
Fat, polite, who had inadvertently gone astray."

So the wolf has a real dog's life: he has no food and doesn't really do what he wants. He's obviously seen some food, but the guard dogs won't let him go near it. In a sense, this wolf's miserable existence is bound to make him unhappy. The dog he meets, on the other hand, seems to have everything he wants, a true Rinti dog, "free to live his dog's life to the full": powerful and handsome, he has never lacked for anything. In fact, he's always had more than he needed, because he's fat. In short, pleasure in complete freedom. Unlike the wolf, the dog is not a wild animal: it is polite and therefore educated, or rather trained. It's a domestic animal, whose master satisfies its every desire:

"Chicken bones, pigeon bones,
Not to mention many a caress."

Petting! Pets, like dogs and cats, are lucky. Their owners can buy them Sheba "to say I love you". It's even better when it's Eva Longoria, "the new face of the Sheba brand". Cats would buy Whiskas, but since they're as broke as that penniless wolf, they're lucky to find a human to do their shopping for them. Who's the master after all? As Rousseau wrote: "Whoever is master cannot be free, and to reign is to

7. "Pleasure in total freedom."

obey[103]." The master is not really who we think he is. At first glance, the master is the one who gives orders and forces his slave to do what he wants: "Sit! Down!" As for the slave, he's not free: he's subject to his master's wishes and must obey him. But when you find yourself having to take the dog out to relieve himself and buy him his Rinti while he stays at home, which of the two is the master?

In the rest of the fable, the dog takes pity on the wolf and offers to take him with him to live under the same roof. But *along the way,* the wolf notices the marks on the dog's neck:

What's that?" he said. - Nothing there. - What's that? Nothing, eh? - Not much.
- But still? - The collar I'm tied to What you see may be the cause.
- Tied up? said the Wolf: don't you run wherever you want? - Not always, but who cares?
- It matters so much that of all your meals
I don't want any part of it,
And wouldn't want even that much treasure.
With that, Master Wolf took off, and ran again."

In a way, then, the dog is happier than the wolf: his master pleases him and satisfies all his desires. It's all the more pleasant because the dog doesn't have to take care of its own needs. But at the same time, he's not free: he's dependent on

103. ROUSSEAU, *Lettres écrites de la Montagne, op. cit.* pages 841-842.

his master and must obey him. The wolf has a much harder life, but he's not dependent on anyone. So how can the dog not realize that he's not free? Precisely because he confuses freedom with pleasure: doing what he wants, and satisfying his every desire. Freedom," writes Rousseau, "consists less in doing one's own will than in not being subject to that of others. But the dog is subject to his master's will. As for the wolf, he doesn't always do what he wants because he doesn't necessarily have the means, but at least he doesn't obey anyone. In short, a life of pleasure is not necessarily free, and those who please us can be our masters, even if they tell us I love you. Monoprix, "What can we do for you today?" Nothing! I'll take care of it.

Spinoza's stone

One morning, in the middle of the week, I happened to stumble upon "Les feux de l'amour" because I was sick. "Who the hell watches that?" I asked myself. In fact, you only have to wait for the ads to find out: Stana stairlifts, Audika hearing aids - "of course" - and even *funeral* agreements from Pompes Funèbres Générales. So, the advertisers seem to know that it's mainly pensioners who watch this - and sick people. At least, that's what the advertisers think they know, as they target their spots to the segment of the population that's supposed to be in front of the TV.

Here again, advertising is based on *science,* and in particular on the human sciences such as sociology. Founded in particular by Émile Durkheim, sociology tends to show that

7. "Pleasure in total freedom."

individuals are subject to social laws, just as things in nature can be subject to physical laws. When a stone is thrown, it falls back at a certain speed, obeying the law of falling bodies. So it's not the stone that decides. Similarly, sociology tells us that the behavior of individuals does not really depend on themselves, but rather on the society in which they live or the social group to which they belong - old, young, *housewives under 50,* etc. Each of us undoubtedly believes we're following our own *path,* as Alfa Romeo Mito or Philips razors would say: "Be proud, if by your actions, from the most discreet to the craziest, you've broken the codes". I probably think I'm getting married because I've met the love of my life, having children because I want to, and buying L'Oréal "because I'm worth it". The truth is, we're often subjected to *codes,* or rather, social rules, without even realizing it. "We can no more choose the shape of our houses than we can choose the shape of our clothes", writes Durkheim: "it's because there's a current of opinion, a collective push that imposes on individuals" [104] their choices, as revealed by those famous statistics denounced by a Meetic ad. "Normally and according to the statistics, I should meet a boy my own age or thereabouts. And normally, and according to the statistics, he should be doing pretty much the same thing as me in life". In short, everyone behaves in the same way under the same conditions.

104. Durkheim (E.), *The Rules of Sociological Method,* chapter one, PUF, "Quadrige", 1996, page 13.

Of course, I think I'm free, like the stone imagined by Spinoza, who doesn't see that it was I who threw it and that it's subject to the law of falling bodies: it "will believe that it is very free and that it perseveres in its movement only because it wants to."[105] But we can very well be subject to laws without realizing it. And if advertising can succeed in defining *targets* or *niches* among consumers, it's because we obey *norms*. And behind this call to *break codes*, advertising hopes above all that we will conform. It necessarily assumes that we are not free: if millions are spent on advertising, it's because it must have a predictable effect on the consumer, just as physical law can have an effect on stone. That's the logic of *marketing*: to study the market, consumer tastes and preferences. If we couldn't predict their behavior, it would be pointless to try and induce people to buy this or that product, like throwing a stone to make it fall. In short, if people were truly free, advertising wouldn't exist.

The Marlboro cowboy

I'm talking about a time no one under twenty could possibly know: Marlboro posters featuring a cowboy. On the posters, as far as I can remember, he was with his horse in the middle of the wide open spaces of the Far West, under a setting sun. Ah! The great outdoors! Wide open spaces are a symbol of freedom, and so is this lone cowboy, far from *codes*, plotting

105. SPINOZA, *Œuvres 4, Traité politique, Lettres*, Lettre LVIII, translated from Latin by C. Appuhn, GF-Flammarion, 1966, page 304.

7. "Pleasure in total freedom."

his own course. And yet, it's an advert for cigarettes that are highly addictive and cause cancer. So we're selling addiction with images of freedom. Once you've understood that, you've understood advertising in general, and advertising for freedom in particular. An image, an illusion. And banning this kind of advertising is an attempt to get us out of the cave. After that, you can prefer smoking - like me: you can prefer pleasure to freedom, but you mustn't confuse the two.

8. "Because you're worth it."

(Who am I?)

"The self *is hateful."*
PASCAL.

"Nespresso. *What else*?" What else? "Madrange: my star ham", and "L'Oréal, because I'm worth it", with Elnett, "La laque des stars". It remains to be seen whether using "La laque des stars" is enough to become one. And Madrange? Ham certainly has many virtues. But lost in the fridge under cellophane paper between leftover pasta and pâté, how does my slice of ham make me a star?

Ah! The stars! The stars, the famous or the "*people*", as if those who aren't famous weren't people at all. The life of the stars is the model of a successful life, not only because they have everything to be happy, like money and the famous villa, but above all, because they have fame. "We are not content with the life we have in ourselves and in our own being," Pascal writes, "we want to live in other people's idea of an imaginary life, and for that we strive to appear." Apparently, it's not so much what we are *in our own being*

8. "Because you're worth it."

that gives us our value: our opinions, our personality traits or our work - in short, what we've done with our lives. Lindsay Lohan or Paris Hilton are "*people*" simply because they appear in magazines. I couldn't tell you what they do - who's Lindsay Lohan, anyway? Basically, they do nothing, which doesn't stop them from being very important people. Their value lies in the number of people who know them and find them important.

Of course, using a celebrity to sell a product allows you to identify your image with that of the brand. When George Clooney uses Nespresso, or rather, when Nespresso uses George Clooney, the machine is associated with everything the actor stands for: glamour, seduction, good looks, his films and even his left-wing political commitments - or rather, the *show* he puts on of his commitments in *an imaginary life* that exists only *in the minds of others*, the public, because in the meantime, he's doing the advertising. The Nespresso coffee maker now carries all the qualities and values that, *in* people's *minds* and *imaginations,* are those of George Clooney. It's Marx's famous *fetishism.* But if advertising uses stars, it's also and above all to highlight the consumer himself. "We're so presumptuous that we'd like to be known by the whole world. So advertising suggests we buy the products of stars.

"L'Oréal: because you're worth it. Let's not forget that the original idea was to sell a shampoo. So we could have just given information like, "it washes your hair", "it eliminates dandruff" or even "it gives you beautiful hair". Then it's up to you to decide if you think it's useful. After all, that's what *marketing is all about*: studying the market, knowing consumers' needs and desires, and producing objects and services that meet their demands. In theory, that is. As everyone knows - we don't believe in Santa Claus anymore - marketing is more about creating demand or need through advertising. "If you don't come to Lagardère, Lagardère will come to you! If I've never taken a trip to the other side of the world, if I've never owned an iPhone or a Nespresso coffeemaker, how could I know that I should miss them - or should I miss them at all? Hence this debauchery of *pleasure, happiness, freedom* and all the other goodies their gizmos are supposed to bring us. But even that's outdated. Kellogg's or L'Oréal don't even talk about their products any more - if only to attribute completely *irrelevant* virtues to them, such as *opening up to others* thanks to Nescafé. Advertising is about me, the consumer, and for some, it has moved "from customer-king to customer-me", from product marketing to "customer marketing" [106].

"Why can't we be friends?"

"The nature of self-love and of this human *self* is to love only oneself and to consider only oneself." And advertisers understand this. They may or may not have read Pascal. In any case, their flattery fits in well with the prevailing individualism. IPC computers: "Too bad for the others. You're right." Nice...

---

106. KAUFMAN (H.) and FAGUER (L.), *Le marketing de l'ego. Du client-roi au client-moi*, chapter 1, Maxima, Laurent Du Mesnil éditeur, 2005, page 44.

8. "Because you're worth it."

Of course, one of the most enduring myths in advertising is that of living together, in which "everyone is beautiful, everyone is nice". Team spirit, solidarity and tribe are constantly extolled in ads where there's always a guy with dreadlocks. In fact, this is the main argument behind the means of *communication* offered by new technologies: iPhone, Internet, telephone, digital cameras, etc. Nokia. "*Connecting people*". And Kodak, "We have so much to share" or "All your emotions are shared in images." In a Bouygues Telecom ad, all the people in the phonebook of a certain "Mathieu" cross paths and talk to each other in the middle of a large green field, with a cheerful, bucolic song in the background: "*Why can't we be friends*?" Except that, in reality, these people don't see each other, don't live together: they're just names in a telephone directory.

One day when I arrived at one of those famous parties where you don't know anyone, a girl came up to me and said:

- Is that you, Gaétan?

- No," I answer. Who's Gaétan?

- A friend.

- Well, you seem to know your friend pretty well.

- Yes, but no, he's a Facebook friend. I've never actually seen him.

"We have so much to share." But what? After all, these technological tools are just means of communication, like speech or mail. And just because we talk to each other doesn't mean we're *friends*: I can very well talk to someone to give them orders, hurl horrors at them or even say nothing at all. And

I can very well send a letter of denunciation or write two banalities on a postcard: "The weather's fine. Kisses." The question is, what messages can these tools exchange? And most of the time, it doesn't go very far. On Facebook, *friends* are often strangers with whom communication is reduced to little more than a "*poke*" and a "*like*" to indicate that we like or agree with each other. And if not, can you elaborate?

You only have to walk around to see that these tools tend to kill communication - obviously. When two people are sitting on a café terrace without talking to each other, each consulting their *apps* on their phones, where's the communication? In the street, people pass or bump into each other without looking at each other, eyes glued to their Smartphones, ears plugged by their earphones. On *public* transport, it's the same: everyone stays in their own world, no doubt posting an essential message on their Facebook page or contemplating their profile photo. SFR, "With my mobile, I'm the star on Facebook. And on the train, they shout out their private, intimate conversations over the phone. "I'm on the train." Isn't this a way of breaking off all communication with those who are there? We're not friends at all: we're disturbing each other. The cell phone makes you totally blind and deaf to the presence of others: you behave with them as if they weren't there. "Because in this case, it's not my comfort that's at stake, it's my very reality. Those who phone on the train "don't just disturb me," remarks Finkielkraut, "they erase me.[107] In short, the

107. Finkielkraut (Alain), *L'imparfait du présent*, Gallimard, 2002, page 111.

8. "Because you're worth it."

means of communication are often obstacles to communication. Some people have understood this, like this Smartphone brand, which almost apologizes in its TV ad: "We are the ones who don't need to be together to be together". Bravo! Give me your method.

Why can't we be friends? Because the consumer society promotes individualism, and advertising encourages it. To present its *e-commerce,* Visa talks about "contactless and mobile payment". Contactless: the dream. It's the same dream we're offered in the ad for online bank BforBank, where "ma banquière, c'est moi" ("my banker is me"). A chilling, black-and-white ad in which a woman finds herself alone in the world on her boat in the middle of nowhere. "I know what you're thinking," she says, "but what's this girl got that I haven't got with her boat?"

"Love one another."

One day, I caught my parents putting Christmas presents under the tree, and I realized that Santa Claus didn't exist. In any case, I more or less knew it already, without admitting it to myself or telling them. In fact, for a year or two, I *pretended to* my parents that I still believed in Santa Claus, so as not to upset them. But deep down, maybe I just didn't want to give up the pleasure of seeing them so attentive to *me,* when they were trying so hard.

And advertising is like parents: I don't really believe what it says, but I love that it's so interested in me. Jean Baudrillard, in particular, draws this parallel between "the logic of Santa Claus" and advertising[108]. Of course we don't believe all these arguments and promises! After seeing all the posters that pollute our landscape, the tunnels of ads that cut off films on TV and the spam that prevents us from reading a page on the Internet, we know it's not true. We're used to it by now: we know we'll never get an orgasm from eating yoghurt, and that "coffee named desire" is a bit of an exaggeration. We also know that all this *freedom* and *happiness* we're promised is just a Com. Opening a Coca-Cola isn't opening happiness: it's just opening Coca-Cola. But as Baudrillard says, "without believing" in the product, "I believe in the advertising that wants me to believe[109]". Because I'm worth it.

Kellogg's *Special K* is without doubt the worst of the customer marketing genre. A cereal with real chocolate chips that won't make you fat - always, "pleasure with freedom". And the slogans compete in *narcissistic perversion*: "you're special and it shows", "Spécial K, the program that loves you", and above all, "love yourself". So hard! I don't know if I could do it. As if I didn't love myself enough already. As Pascal remarks, it's in everyone's nature "to love only oneself and to consider only oneself[110]". Why is that? It's hard to say. It's a natural law. According to Freud, auto-eroticism or narcissism

---

108. BAUDRILLARD (Jean), *Le système des objets*, D, III, la publicité, Gallimard, "TEL", 1968, page 232.

109. *Ibid.*

110. PASCAL, *Pensées*, 100, GF-Flammarion, 1976, page 79.

8. "Because you're worth it."

is the first form of sexuality experienced by the child[111]. He pleases himself alone and "satisfies himself by means of his own body"[112]. This is the first phase in the construction of an individual's sexuality and personality. Autoeroticism, from the Greek "*erôs*", love, and *auto*, self, corresponds exactly to the Kelloggian imperative: "love yourself". Except that this narcissism stems from the most primal instinct, and there's no need to add to it. On the contrary, the education that parents give their children should lead them to be a little less navel-gazing in order to adapt to the world and to society. A child would like to satisfy all his whims, but his parents must teach him that this is not always possible, and that sometimes it's wrong, by instilling in him feelings "like shame, disgust, morality". According to Freud, the *normal* evolution of the child leads him to *overcome* his narcissism and turn his love towards someone other than himself. Otherwise, there's a problem. Those who have not gone beyond the stage of auto-eroticism in adulthood suffer from *infantilism*, or even *perversion*. Only a *pervert* seeks his own pleasure without taking others into account, except to treat them as mere *things* to satisfy his desires - before throwing them away.

"Special K, love yourself!" And Pentax: "You're talented." Hyundai, "You've got it all figured out" or Estée Lauder: "Only

---

111. Narcissus is a character from Greek mythology who fell in love with his own reflection. Staring at his image in the water, he falls and drowns.
112. FREUD, *Five Lessons on Psychoanalysis*, Lesson Four, *op. cit.* page 63.See also, FREUD, *Pour introduire au narcissisme*, translated from the German by O. Mannoni, Petite Bibliothèque Payot, 2012.

you know what's really important." In all cases, advertising treats the consumer like a kid, infantilizing him by keeping him in the narcissistic phase of sexuality. It's all very well to tell your little one that the noodle necklace he brought home for Mother's Day is very pretty, or that his drawing is beautiful. But at some point, you also have to teach him to grow up. Obviously, a brand can only please the consumer by flattering his *ego*. For is it not true," writes Pascal, "that we hate the truth and those who tell it to us, and that we like them to be mistaken to our advantage? But you have to admit, this is argumentation at its worst.

"We don't have the same values."

"L'Oréal: because you're worth it." Why, *because*? I can make myself a cup of coffee *because* I'm thirsty, or wash my hair because it's dirty. But what's the causal link between a shampoo and my self-worth? I'm an exceptional person, *so* I use L'Oréal.[113] A new version of Descartes' *cogito*: "I think, therefore I am", like all the ads that claim to answer the famous question: "Who am I?" Not only shampoos and hair colorings, but also Coca-Cola, which doesn't always bet on happiness: Coca-Cola light, "Really myself." In relation to what? Of course, fashion accessories such as clothes and jewelry are also important: "Agatha c'est moi" (Agatha is

113. In the same vein: *Werther's Original*: "Because you're an exceptional person." But then again, what do butterscotch candies have to do with my self-worth?

8. "Because you're worth it."

me), "en Devernois, je suis moi" (I am me in Devernois). But even cell phone ads have given up on playing on the famous *communication*: it's not for others, but for yourself that you should buy a cell phone, because it's less about *connecting people* than distinguishing them. The aim is not to communicate with others, but to express one's personality: LG Optimus (GT540), "my personality, my mobile, my apps". And again, SFR: "Definitely me. On days that are absolutely me. Me, me, me, always me. But "What is *me*?" asks Pascal.

Is my mobile "just me"? Yet I can lose my mobile or my apps, "without losing myself". If I change my phone, I probably won't change at all: I'll still be me - with another phone. Consciousness cannot be personalized in an object," writes Baudrillard, "it's absurd", because I'm *definitely* not a phone. When we say: "I'd like you to love me for what I am", do we mean: "I'd like you to love me for my car or my apps"? On the contrary, we think that who I am has nothing to do with all the material objects I own. "Where is this "me"? What makes me me? "In Devernois, I'm me. And *not in* Devernois? I'll still be me, except I'll be dressed differently. It's probably not the way I look that makes me me. Of course, the way you dress can be a way of *giving yourself* personality. But is it really *essential*? When we say: "I'd like you to love me for what I am", it's because we refuse to be loved or looked at for our physical qualities. When it comes down to it, my body isn't really me. Even Special K from Kellog's understands this: the famous TV ad that ends with the slogan "aimez-vous" ("love yourself") speaks of the body as an object outside and different from myself: "We've seen it grow, and we've seen it change. We've hidden it, we've controlled it. We've loved it, we've forgotten it... and what if we decided to live another relationship with our body?" I *see* my body growing, as if it were in front of me, because it's not really me. So where is this *on* that looks at its body as another? What am I? A spirit, of course. What I am is inside. In fact, *personality* refers to psychological or moral qualities, such as intelligence, selfishness or generosity. This is what Descartes' famous *cogito* means in the first place: "I think, therefore I am". It's the way I think that defines my personality. For Descartes, before being a body and, above all, a telephone, "I am a thinking thing". It's my mind - or my state of mind - that makes me who I am.

That said, "what's done on the inside shows on the outside", as Bio from Danone, now Activia, used to say. If I change my phone or my clothes, I'll still be me, but what if I change my body? If I wake up one morning looking like someone else, it won't really be me that I see. As Descartes himself recognized: "I am not only lodged in my body as a pilot in his ship". When I look at myself in the mirror, it's really me that I see, and after talking about the body in such a strange way, Kellog's still ends up saying, "Love yourself!" You are your body. My outward appearance is therefore part of me, and the way I dress is a way of expressing my personality: it even reflects my way of thinking, my tastes, my social status and even, why not, my political opinions. "In Devernois, I am me".

Is it really so absurd, then, that consciousness should become personified in an object? After all, Jean Baudrillard

8. "Because you're worth it."

himself acknowledges that there is a *system of objects that can* never be reduced to their primary function or utility: there is a "lived psychological and sociological reality of objects". I don't buy a smartphone simply because I need to make a phone call - of course. It's also, and above all, to show who I am: young, active, at the cutting edge of technology, "CSP+", and so on. The "object system" is Bordeau Chesnel logic: "We don't have the same values". At first glance, it seems ridiculous to want to assert one's social status through a jar of pork rillettes. But this is how we experience our relationship with all objects: we don't just buy them for their usefulness, but above all, to say something about ourselves. Diet Coke: "really myself". Of course I'm not a bottle of Coke. It's just that people who drink Diet Coke are "natural", authentic people who don't care what anyone says. People who drink Pepsi, on the other hand, are notorious hypocrites.

"Ultra-customizable"

One day, I made the FATAL mistake *of* going to a shopping area on a Sunday to visit Ikea, or rather Alinéa, the Ikea for the poor - even though Ikea is already reserved for the very middle classes. It's much the same: families dragging their feet and jostling each other in the aisles to look at the models on display. It's the weekend's cultural outing: just like at a museum, there's an "exhibition" and an itinerary signposted "next visit". Except that these are not works of art, for the good reason that each piece of furniture is manufactured in dozens of copies - although *manufactured is a misnomer,* since you have to assemble it yourself. In the end, everyone buys the same sofa bed or the famous "*STEN*" shelf. So, during my initiatory circumambulations in this temple of consumerism, I was curious enough to approach a bed on display. I was astonished to read the store's slogan on the label: "Alinéa, for a home that's just like you". Because if my Alinéa or Ikea home only looks like me, it's because I look like everyone else.

An advert for the Citroën DS3 uses a black-and-white image from the famous series "Alfred Hitchcock Presents". The master of suspense says: "I wanted to tell you that I'm fed up with black", because black and white is uniform and monotonous, whereas the DS3 offers a wide choice of *pop*, bright, acid or *flashy* colors. So it's "ultra-customizable". *Personalizing* your car means making it unique, so that you can stand out from the crowd. And if the DS3 is "ultra-customizable", it's because there are *even more* colors than for other models. But is it enough to have a car color or smartphone "app" that's different from the others to have personality?

Of course not. Jean Baudrillard points out that these are entirely superficial, even illusory ways of distinguishing oneself from others, because the color of a car "is a marginal difference", "or rather an inessential difference"[114]. Firstly, because color is not an essential characteristic of the car itself: whether yellow or blue, it will never be anything

114. BAUDRILLARD (Jean), *Le système des objets*, D, I, *op. cit.*, page 198.

8. "Because you're worth it."

other than a Citroën DS3 with the same engine - and the same price. Ultimately, if I wanted to distinguish myself from others through a car, I could at least buy one that was truly different, like a Ferrari or a Rolls Royce - why not. As Baudrillard reminds us, there aren't many colors of Rolls Royce, there's only one - black - and that's how you recognize them. Besides, a canary-yellow or apple-green Rolls wouldn't look like anything, and would be a bit of a departure from the character it's supposed to represent: aristocratic and tasteful. If I've reduced myself to one color to differentiate myself, it's because for the rest, I had neither the means nor even the idea of buying a car other than the one everyone else had. In the end, my DS3 shows that I belong to the middle class and that I'm "ultra-conformist". When you've got a Rolls, you don't need to distinguish yourself by color. And even if I really wanted to distinguish myself from others through my relationship with these *technical objects that are means of transport,* I'd have to get rid of the tyranny of the car and choose another vehicle like the train or bicycle. In the end, the invasive discourse of the customer-me is itself an illusion, since the aim is to sell millions of copies of the same thing, whether car or smartphone - if I were the only customer of Citroën or SFR, they'd have gone out of business a long time ago. They defend individualism, but push us to conformism. I think I distinguish myself not only by buying the same car as everyone else, but above all, by buying a car: "I buy, therefore I am". A BMW slogan claims, "You've never let anyone dictate your tastes. You've done the right thing." Not true. "The mere fact of choosing this or that object to distinguish yourself from others is in itself a social service". This is Jean Baudrillard quoting John Stuart Mill. And it's so true!

"That's all I love!" (Padam Pam Pam Pam)

It's important not to let your tastes be dictated to, because that's the only way to be "truly yourself", as the American philosopher Coca-Cola would say. That's probably also what Hugo Boss' strange slogan means: "your rules of the game". Which game? Surely that social game in which everyone tries to find their place or their "differentiation", in order to answer the question "who am I?". But Hugo Boss or BMW are lying. These rules of the game aren't mine, they're the rules of the consumer society that manages to get it into our heads that the only way to define oneself or assert one's personality is to buy all their products - cars, perfumes, telephones, etc. Besides, if Hugo Boss tells me what perfume to wear, I don't see how it could be *my perfume*. For that, I'd have to make it myself, incorporating the scents I love because they remind me of my childhood, and in particular, the smell of the fields at Limésy, near Rouen. That's what I like. I like to feel my fingertips, too. I often look at myself in the mirror, not at all to admire myself, but to make sure I don't look sick. And if there's one thing I hate, it's when someone says to me: "Are you all right? You look white." Nothing makes me feel worse. I'm just saying, I don't know how Hugo Boss could know all that.

After all, I'm in the best position to know myself. This is also what Descartes meant with his famous "I think, therefore I

8. "Because you're worth it."

am": "I see clearly that there is nothing easier for me to know than my mind[115]". It's not always easy to know what other people are thinking: I'm not inside their heads, and I can only trust what they tell me - "that's all I like". I can also try to interpret their gestures, mimics or facial expressions, but I can always be wrong - "Are you all right? Say, you're white - no, I'm fine, I assure you - no, because really, you're white." But if I can't guess what the other person is thinking, he knows exactly what he's thinking. Just as I know exactly what's in my head. And yet, advertising would know me better than I know myself, by revealing to me what my desires and thoughts are, as in the famous "I dreamt it, Sony did it!" And McDonald's: "it's everything I love", and Windows 7, "it was my idea". The advertiser still thinks he's a philosopher, applying the famous motto of Socrates inscribed on the pediment of the Delphic oracle: "Know thyself". Rather than giving information about the product, advertising gives the customer information about himself, claiming to precede his desires without him having expressed them, and without him even knowing them. Except that in "know thyself", there's "know thyself", but there's also "thyself". By claiming to reveal me to myself, *customer marketing* has no other aim than to *dictate my tastes*.

At the same time, it's true that I don't really know why I like smelling my fingertips: there's a little smell that reassures me. Freud would no doubt see this as the return of repressed

115. DESCARTES, *Méditations métaphysiques*, Méditation seconde, Nathan, "Les Intégrales de Philo", 1999, page 67.

childhood desires linked to "coprophilic pleasures of childhood, i.e. those related to excrement[116]". Unlike Descartes, psychoanalysis hypothesizes the Unconscious, and assumes that I don't know myself as well as I think I do. This is the meaning of all these remarks on self-eroticism and children's sexual desires: each of us is said to be driven by desires we don't know about, the very desires we had to repress when our parents taught us "shame, disgust, morality": "Daddy, what's that bottle of milk? Daddy, how do you make babies?" But *repressed* doesn't mean *disappeared*. The "repressed" homosexual refuses to satisfy his sexual tendencies, which doesn't mean they're not still there, even if he's not really aware of it. In addition to being a philosopher, the advertising executive is also a psychoanalyst. But the aim of psychoanalysis is to heal, or at least to treat the sick, to free them from their neuroses *through reflection*. By becoming aware of their desires, patients gain a better understanding of what's wrong with them: "psychoanalytic treatment responds to the highest ambitions of intellectual and moral life." And advertising? It's more a response to the demands of soap salesmen, which aren't very high: to get us to buy their salads, Big Macs, perfumes and shampoos.

"What else?"

Stars have the life everyone dreams of, and no one will ever have. Money, fame, villas with swimming pools, travel, etc.

116. FREUD, *Five Lessons on Psychoanalysis*, *op. cit.*, page 66.

8. "Because you're worth it."

As Guy Debord says in *La Société du Spectacle*, stars embody "the unattainable result of social labor[117]". Most people have to work hard to earn a living, and when you're at work, all you're looking forward to is the weekend or a vacation. That's when you're really happy: you can finally spend your money and do what you want. The life of a star is therefore an ideal life: for them, it's vacations all year round. Don't they?

No. In fact, stars are paid to show us what we should dream of, through those clichés of happiness to which we should all conform. The star is the model of the happy life in consumer society. They make everyone believe that happiness is all about consumption. According to Guy Debord, the star is "the enemy of the individual"[118]. Firstly, because they remind everyone in front of the TV that they've really missed out on life. Secondly, because it prevents each and every one of us from seeking our own definition of happiness, and making a life of our own. So *what else* can we dream of?

---

117. Debord (Guy), *La Société du Spectacle*, III, §60, *op. cit.*, page 55.
118. *Ibid*, III, §61, page 56.

9. "Don't get old too fast."

(Does it make sense to want to escape time?)

"Don't forget that the devil is old,
so get old yourself so you can understand him."
Max Weber.

One of the ugliest campaigns I know is Orangina's, with its garish colors and monstrous animals with humanoid, highly "sexualized" bodies: the bear putting on deodorant and the giraffe hanging out its laundry with Orangina detergent, "naturally". There's nothing natural about it, of course. But why show such repulsive images for an ad? Why create discomfort when the aim is to make consumers *want to* buy a product? Of course, it's because we've reached the *nec plus ultra* of "conceptual" advertising, which has long since gone beyond simple advertising to become a work of art. This twilight Orangina campaign claims that advertising has gone beyond art, and art has gone beyond advertising. The product? There's no need to present it any more: what's the point of talking about that little yellow bottle that has to be shaken, "otherwise the pulp stays at the bottom". Like many of the advertising slogans we all have in our heads, Orangina slogans are part of the collective memory or unconscious - "But why is he so mean? Because!" Advertising has long since become part of our cultural heritage. "If brands are not products, but ideas, attitudes, values and experiences, why shouldn't they also constitute a culture[119]?" This is exactly what these ads show, where the Orangina bottle can just as easily become deodorant for bears or washing powder for giraffes. The message is clear: I'm such a well-known brand that it's pointless explaining to you what I sell. In fact, I'm not selling anything: I'm not a commodity, I'm a "concept" or a work of art. In short, "the brand spreads[120]". And when it comes to art, we've already seen much worse in the assertion of a disturbing aesthetic of the ugly: baroque, surrealism or the tortured paintings of Francis Bacon. It's not beautiful, it's monstrous and therefore, magnificent. This Orangina campaign does indeed provoke those feelings by which Kant defined the Sublime: "*astonishment* bordering on horror, horror and the sacred shudder that seize the spectator[121]."

On the other hand, there's another even uglier campaign, for Virgin radio, "let's stay fresh". And here, even if you go looking for Kant, you have to admit that if this campaign is ugly, it's just because it's completely messed up - and not

119. KLEIN (Naomi), *op. cit.* page 56.
120. *Ibid,* page 53.
121. KANT, *Critique of the Faculty of Judgment,* Part I, Section I, Book II, translated from the German by J.-R. Ladmiral, M.B. de Launay and J.-M. Vaysse, Gallimard, "Folio-Essais", 1985, page 213.

fresh at all. These are the posters that have been hanging around the streets for some time, showing "young people", wrinkled and aged by Photoshop, with the slogan: "Don't age too fast". One shows a girl molded into a denim minishort, with a fluorescent pink belt and a red-striped sailor's jacket revealing her shoulder. She has the body of a half-dressed young virgin, like an appeal to the sexual and slightly pedophilic impulses of those who pass in front of the poster. Except that her face is wrinkled, a bit like aging the photo of a child who disappeared years ago to see what he might look like *now*. The ad therefore displays a necessarily monstrous old age. It's ugly, it's ugly, it's repulsive, the idea being precisely to give an appalling image of old age. In fact, the campaign continued with the relief of a return to *normality* or naturalness: "WITH" Virgin Radio, the girl regains her youthful good looks - phew! It was just a nightmare. The campaign is repeated with two other "young-olds", one guy on a skateboard, the other in a leather jacket, always using the same principle: young clothes and an old face photoshopped with wrinkles. So, of course, a teenage girl with an old man's face is scary. But it's like the *monsters* of Greek mythology, Minotaur, Centaur or Chimera, made up of different animal parts: half man, half bull, lion's head, goat's body and snake's tail. Advertising thus creates a completely artificial image of old age as an anomaly or disease. Of course, there's nothing uglier than an old woman *clinging to* her lost youth by having her skin pulled and dressing like a schoolgirl. You have to tell them one day: when you've had a facelift, you never look

9. "Don't get old too fast."

younger, only *weirder*. So it's not old age itself that's ugly: it's what it becomes for those who seek to escape it. It's better to admit that old age is perfectly natural, because it's the *fear* of growing old that creates monsters.

"Nurture the youth within you."

"Don't get old too fast". I want to, but what can I do about it? There are things that depend on us, and others that don't. Time passes, what do you want? Time passes, what do you want? The only way to avoid aging is to die. When you commit suicide at 15, as the *cool* girl in the Virgin ad should, you know you'll never grow old. Is that what you want? If not, it's a good thing I'm getting old. Every time I celebrate my birthday, I tell myself that at least *I*'ve made it this far!Yes, but no! Don't age too quickly *in your head*! That's what we mean! Stay young!" But why?

It's the *categorical* imperative of advertising: stay young. Escape the passage of time by fighting against old age and aging. Ageing of the body, first of all, with all those creams and products with L'Oréal-style "Revitalift" effects that make wrinkles disappear. It's the Oil of Olaz syndrome: "I'm 50, did you guess it?" But there's more to body maintenance than superficial "cosmetic" touch-ups that only change the outward appearance. You also need to maintain your physical shape from the inside, for example, by drinking Evian water, "declared by your body to be a source of youth". "Maintain the youthfulness within you". - that's an order! I don't see why not. It's undoubtedly preferable not to be diminished, suffering and dependent when you're old, and even the Epicurean philosopher gives this advice to the "old man": "as he grows old, let him remain young[122]". "As for the man who advises the young man to live well and the old man to finish living well, he is stupid[123]". Should we, just because we're old, put our cars away? Should we be content to wait for death with nothing more to look forward to in life, with only the memory of having lived well to console us? Advances in science and medicine are enabling us to live longer, and so much the better. In a TV ad for GAN, the voice of Édouard Baer - a symbol of Parisian hipness - announces: "You liked *Jean-Jacques*, you'll love *Jean-Jacques 2, retirement*! Between his "active" life and his retirement, Jean-Jacques hasn't changed: he's as dynamic as ever. In fact, it's the same actor who plays both - he's just had his hair dyed white. There's no difference between youth and old age. Old people are no longer "3rd age" people, they're "seniors" enjoying life to the full. Isn't it precisely because they were wise enough to prepare for their retirement a long time ago by taking out a policy with GAN? In the words of the philosopher: "For no one is too early or too late when it comes to ensuring the health of the soul[124]". The young, by planning for old age; the senior, by enjoying life.

So it's not just the health of the body that we need to look after, but also that of the soul. Staying young, in the sense of

122. Epicurus, *Letter to Meneca, op. cit.*, page 43.
123. *Ibid*, page 46.
124. *Ibid*, page 43.

9. "Don't get old too fast."

the Virgin ad advising us not to age too quickly: in this case, by listening to young *people's* music on Virgin radio, because Rihanna is fresher than Bach or Mozart, who died a long time ago. "You're not going to listen to old people's music! To be young in spirit is to have young tastes - which presupposes that we know how to define them, and that they're all the same. As in this TV ad for the Citroën DS5 Hybrid & Diesel - another one I hate: we see a symphony orchestra playing - yuck! Classical music! So corny! But as if to thumb one's nose at this old-fashioned music, the hardcore sound of Marilyn Manson is superimposed on the images. And bang! In the teeth! With this slogan as the coup de grâce: "Change the times. That's right! Classical music is dusty! Apart from that, the ad would like to represent "culture"...

To have a young mind, with young tastes and, above all, young morals - which is to say, no morals. Because when it comes to morals, it's young people who have the truth: it's not old people or parents who set the standards for what to do and what to be. It's young people who have figured out everything about life. Hence the "marketing of cool" evoked by Naomi Klein[125]. Many brands are trying to give themselves a "youthful" image, to appeal to young people and thereby explain to them how they should live. "Catch the FANTAttitude!" Everything *must* always be *fun*, cool. "Have fun", a way of understanding the famous *Carpe Diem* (Gather

125. Klein (Naomi), *op. cit.* page 93. See the whole of chapter 3, "Everything is alternative: the youth market and the marketing of cool", pages 93-119.

the day), which sums up Epicurus' philosophy. As in this TV ad for M6 Mobile, a not-too-distant cousin of Virgin radio: a young man surrounded by his gang declares that they were sick and tired of not being able to live together - because that, too, is FUN. So they decided to find a great apartment to bring all their buddies into: "the concept worked pretty well" - another concept. Then another young man takes us on a tour of the premises, where some play table soccer, others make music. With the killer slogan: "You've got the profile. And if you don't, you haven't understood a thing about life! There's only one *model of* life, and it's an imposed figure of happiness: that of young people who live in gangs or "tribes". If you're alone, you must be unhappy, and if you're "old", you must bow to this youthful morality. Thus, in a Renault ad that touches the abyssal depths of stupidity, a mother picks up her daughter from school in a Twingo. The girl gets into the passenger seat, and the mother notices a tattoo on her lower back: "What's that?! exclaims the mother, apparently shocked. Apparently: in fact, the mother pulls up her sweater and shows her daughter that she also has an even bigger tattoo: "that's a tattoo!" Wow! What a cool mom! She's awesome! She's not a mother, she's a real girlfriend with a young spirit who understands everything about life. She's "right with the times, right in her Twingo". She doesn't scold her daughter like an old *maid* who had the misfortune of trying to educate her child. In short, one more ad to be awarded a prize at the Conservatoire des étalons de la connerie universelle.

9. "Don't get old too fast."

"The president is baby."

Growing old is not a disease: not only because it's the natural course of events, but also because time doesn't always destroy, it also builds. "Don't grow old too fast". But aging also means growing and maturing. It's strange that we think of old age only as a loss, without realizing that time spent can lead to the acquisition of knowledge and know-how. Isn't old age also wisdom? Even Nutella, the favorite brand of dirty kids, knows this: "25 years of experience will always make the difference." So, perhaps the "old" has something to teach the "young". Education is an art," writes Kant, "the practice of which must be perfected through many generations[126]". Educating children means first and foremost *instructing* them and imparting knowledge, which undoubtedly enables them to reach the "age of reason", by being less naive and gullible. Each of us is not born into a world devoid of everything: I inherit the knowledge acquired by previous generations. Today's schoolchildren, for example, learn that the earth revolves around the sun, not the other way around. They grow up in a world where new truths have already been discovered, and don't have to start from scratch. Educating a child also means teaching him the *discipline* that "transforms animality into humanity[127]". Because

126. KANT, *Propos de pédagogie*, introduction, translated from the German by P. Jalabert, in *Œuvres philosophiques*, III, Gallimard, "Bibliothèque de la Pléiade", 1986, page 1153.
127. *Ibid*, 1149.

a child is undoubtedly not reasonable: he simply follows his desires and instincts, without really being aware of what he's doing. As Epicurus says, he may not be aware that we must sometimes "leave aside many pleasures, when the result for us is more unpleasantness[128]". If I eat too much chocolate, I'll get sick. Conversely, "not all suffering is by nature to be refused[129]". Even if it hurts to go to the dentist, you still have to go *for your own good,* otherwise it will be worse. But this skilful calculation between good and bad pleasures requires a little experience and wisdom. For a child, there's nothing obvious about it: if he could, he'd pounce on all the sweets on the supermarket shelves like misery on the world. It's up to his parents to reason with him and not give in to his whims when he demands something.

And yet, it's only in those famous ads for cheeses and good old-fashioned products like Lepetit or Saint-Albray that we still see fathers passing on their experience or know-how to their children. But that's a thing of the past. Today, it's the children who teach their parents about life. It's the mother who has to adopt her daughter's lifestyle, under the guise of staying *young* and *cool.* Generations have nothing to pass on to each other: "old people" or parents have nothing to teach their children, because they're supposed to be more ignorant than they are. All they need to know is how to use all the features of the new iPhone 5G or the new Windows. And in

128. Epicurus, *Letter to Meneca, op. cit.,* page 48.
129. *Ibid,* page 49.

9. "Don't get old too fast."

this respect, it's young people who have things to teach their parents, who are always *behind the times* and *more in the know*. The generation gap is just a gulf, a barrier of incomprehension for which the parent is solely to blame, as soon as he or she is not "in tune with the times". There's no point in making your children listen to Mozart, the Doors or even Pearl Jam, which has already become "*Old School*". It's not the time anymore, and if they don't like it, they're right. As Nestlé says: "The president is baby". It's not up to children to submit their desires to their parents' reason; it's up to parents to submit their reason to their children's desires. Because children are the ideal target for the consumer society: naive, they believe everything they're told, and want to satisfy all their desires. So values have to be reversed: parents must obey their children, and if you don't, you're not cool! It's the child-king, of course, as in the advert I hate most, the one for Nutella: "for all the things they're going to do today: play, learn, have fun". Mind you, they're mostly having fun, and not learning much. The main thing is to buy them Nutella. "It takes a lot of energy to be a spoiled brat.

"Change the times."

Is Marilyn Manson necessarily better than classical music? That's debatable. "To each his own, if you like. But the tyranny of youth and modernity doesn't assert that all tastes are equal. The new is always better than the old, simply because it's new. In fact, it's not so much the tyranny of modernity as the tyranny of fashion. "No, not everything was better before", as the slogan of another youth radio station, Le Mouv, proclaims: it's possible to believe in progress, and that's why time can be constructive. Prehistoric man or the Vikings may have already eaten Apéricubes, but they must also have had somewhat Spartan living conditions, put a lot on their faces and treated their wives with less respect than they do today - perhaps, no? But if things have changed, if a few technical and scientific advances have brought us out of the caves, if any legal advances have given women a few rights, it's all thanks to past history. "One generation educates the other[130]", wrote Kant. Imagine that humanity resembled a three-week-old rabbit, and that no history preceded us: what would modernity have to do with it? Nothing: we'd be living in the wild, without water or electricity, and worse, without Nutella. Modernity is the *current* era, which is modern and *advanced* only thanks to the efforts of previous eras. Modernity is the present thanking the past for what it has given it, and without which it would not be what it is: cars, iPhones, etc. These technological "innovations" didn't happen overnight. In short, modernity is a continuation of progress that took time.

Nothing to do with fashion, which claims a radical break with the past: "change the times". It's not better because it's better than the previous one: it's better because it's new. This is the logic of the consumer society: "everything must go. To consume is to destroy: when I consume a food, I use it and

130. KANT, *Propos de pédagogie, op. cit.* page 1150.

9. "Don't get old too fast."

then it no longer exists, digested by the gastric juices of my stomach and the villi of my small intestine. For us to buy the latest Gillette fusion Proglide, the old Gillette Mach 3 had to be good to go, even though it was sold as "masculine perfection" at the time - so it wasn't all that perfect. Jean Baudrillard underlines the efforts of manufacturers to produce ever newer, ever more efficient objects, and even the manufacturing secrets that intentionally limit the life expectancy of objects. We make them so that they don't last, so that they break down, and the consumer is forced to buy more. And if they don't, we distill this advertising rhetoric about "staying young" and always in fashion. You see: I've barely bought my iPhone 3G when it's already been overtaken by a 4G, and if I want to stay fashionable, cool and up to date, I have to buy the latest model. So we want to stay young to escape the passage of time, whereas it's our consumption habits that throw us into the perpetual renewal of ephemeral objects of which there's never anything left.

"Bon vivant rhymes with foresight" (but with other things too)

What if I were to tell you that Epicurus recommends that young people remain old in spirit? But that's exactly what he says: "that, however young he may be, he may be an *old man* by his lack of fear of what is to come" [131]. What will happen? Time will pass, we'll grow old and die. So we have to be "old

131. ÉPICURE, Lettre à Ménécée, *op. cit.*, page 43

enough" in our minds: mature enough and wise enough to accept it, and knowing that "there's no escaping it", enjoy the happiness of our youth. On the contrary, while we ask old people to be "seniors" or "old-young", we force young people to think about their retirement, as in this GAN ad where *Jean-Jacques* doesn't enjoy anything after all, because he has to take care of *Jean-Jacques 2* - yes! It's not the end of the story, but it's not the end! As in those TV ads for Crédit Agricole, where real-fake people from everyday life, and in particular cool, fun-loving "young people", admit on camera: "It's true, it's about time I thought about it". Fighting the passage of time, again. Advertising - for insurance, loans and pensions - is invaded by anxiety about the future and desperate attempts to master it. Everywhere, we're asked to maintain our "capital", in other words, to save, hoard and conserve what we have for later. Even in advertisements for yoghurts, which we make our children eat: "You see, this will help you build strong bones". Maintain your "bone capital". But what's the point of saving it for later, if I'm going to die tomorrow morning? What's the point of saying, "when it comes to happiness, the time hasn't come yet[132]". The best of its kind is undoubtedly the famous "convention obsèques", "to leave a small capital to those you love", with the late Jean-Marie Proslier, because "I know that living well rhymes with thinking ahead". But if "death is nothing to us" because we'll no longer be anything, perhaps it's "foolish"

132. *Ibid.*

9. "Don't get old too fast."

to spend our lives, and the little time we have left, thinking about our death.

In the end, the famous *young people* are very old indeed, since they're already thinking about the time of their death. In this desperate and pointless attempt to escape time, everyone misses out on life. The young, because they're afraid of growing old, and instead of taking advantage of life's "fruits", they start applying anti-wrinkle creams at thirty and sign up for retirement plans at twenty. Old people, because they want to *stay young*. It's hardly surprising, with these dynamic, lively *senior citizens* in advertising, who don't look much like the grannies and grandpas of the real world, herded into retirement homes because they don't *conform*. We "praise seniors" to deny the reality of old age. In a letter to one of his disciples, Epicurus himself refers to "the suffering caused by urine retention and dysentery[133]". But what keeps him, if not young, at least happy, is thinking about the good times of the past, not regretting their loss, but rejoicing in having lived them. If you're going to have a life, you might as well have this one.

---

133. *Ibid*, page 54.

Books recommended by leading brands

Baudrillard (J.), *Le système des objets,* Gallimard, "Tel", 1968.

- *La société de consommation,* Denoël, 1970.

Bénilde (M.), *On achète bien les cerveaux. Advertising and the media,* Raisons d'agir, 2008.

Brune (F.), *Le bonheur conforme,* Gallimard, "Le Monde actuel", 1985.

Cathelat (B.), *Publicité et société,* Petite Bibliothèque Payot, 2001.

Debord (G.), *La Société du Spectacle,* Gallimard, "Folio", 1992.

Deleuze (G.), *Pourparlers (1972-1990),* Les Éditions de Minuit, "Reprise", 2003.

Epicurus, *Lettre à Ménécée,* translated from the Greek by P.-M. Morel, GF-Flammarion, 2009.

Kaufman (H.), Faguer (L.), *Le marketing de l'ego. Du Client-Roi au Client-Moi,* Maxima, 2005.

Klein (N.), *No Logo.* La tyrannie des marques, Actes Sud, 2001.

Mill (J. S.), *Nature,* La découverte/Poche, 2003.

SUESSADA (D.), *La société de consommation de soi,* Verticales, 1999.
- *L'esclavemaître,* Verticales/Le seuil, 2002.
ROULLET (B.), DROULERS (O.), *Neuromarketing. Le marketing revisité par les neurosciences du consommateur,* Dunod, 2010.
SÉNÈQUE, *La vie heureuse, la Brièveté de la vie,* GF-Flammarion, 2005.
- *De la providence, De la constance du sage, De la tranquillité de l'âme, Du loisir,* translated from Latin by P. Miscevic, GF-Flammarion, 2002.
WEBER (M.), *Le savant et le politique,* "Le métier et la vocation de savant", Plon, "10 /18", 1963.

Table of contents

Best sellers Max Milo Editions

Hitler's banker, Jean-François Bouchard

Confessions of a forger, Éric Piedoie Le Tiec

The Koran and the flesh, Ludovic-Mohamed Zahed

Governing by fake news, Jacques Baud

Governing by chaos, Collectif

A political history of food, Paul Ariès

Mad in U.S.A.: The ravages of the "American model", Michel Desmurget

Mondial soccer club geopolitics, Kévin Veyssière

Putin: Game master?, Jacques Braud

Treatise on the three impostors: Moses, Jesus, Muhammad, The Spirit of Spinoza

TV Lobotomy, Michel Desmurget

www.ingramcontent.com/pod-product-compliance
Lightning Source LLC
LaVergne TN
LVHW012054160826
845678LV00014B/2820

* 9 7 8 2 3 1 5 0 1 2 6 2 6 *